To My friends
Taylor & Cla—
Taylor / with best
wishes —

[signature]

Praise for
Selling Value

"*Selling Value* is a timely and needed book written by a true expert on the subject. Don Hutson does a thorough job of teaching the skills needed to thrive in today's competitive selling environment. I enthusiastically recommend this book to all sales professionals whether they are just starting out or seasoned pros."

Mark Sanborn, C.P.A.E.
President, Sanborn & Associates
New York Times bestselling author of *The Fred Factor*

"I have known Don Hutson for over 40 years and his approach to selling is to always sell the value of a product. Whether on the platform or writing, his blueprint for a successful sale is to know your customers and their needs. You will profit from the messages in *Selling Value!*

Dr. Jim Tunney
Former NFL Referee
Speaker
Author of 101 Best of Tunney Side of Sports

"Without exception, the most consistently excellent sales authority is Don Hutson. You can be confident that his new book, *Selling Value*, will provide you with everything you need to sell the value of your products in great abundance!"

Patricia Fripp
Author and Presentation Skills Expert

"You will love the practical insight of Don Hutson in *Selling Value*. Not only has Don been one of America's top sales speakers, trainers, and gurus for decades, he's someone who is involved in selling his company's products and services every day. If anyone asks me how they can improve their sales, I will simply tell them that *Selling Value* is the book to read to make it happen. His experience alone makes this book a *must read!*"

Scott McKain
Hall-of-Fame Speaker
Author of Create Distinction

"How often have you heard...Your price is too high!? Well, maybe it's because the value you created for your product/service in the mind of the customer is too low. Don Hutson's newest book, *Selling Value*, proves yet again why Don is THE master at teaching salespeople how to create product/service value that overshadows price. Goodbye price objections—hello *Selling Value!*"

Dr. Tony Alessandra
Author of *Non-Manipulative Selling*
and *The Platinum Rule for DISC Sales Mastery*

"The only reason anyone buys is to receive Value. Don Hutson is THE leading authority on Selling Value, as you will discover while reading this book. Make *Selling Value* a staple in your business library and your first gift book to new graduates or start-up entrepreneurs. No matter what other sales or marketing books you buy this one will be the foundation from which they are built."

Jim Cathcart
Author of Relationship Selling™
Founder, The Cathcart Institute

"Selling value today is as sophisticated as flying an airplane. You never take off without preparing a flight plan, carefully going through your checklist and measuring your progress to a predetermined destination. In *Selling Value* Don Hutson gives you that flight plan in easy to understand segments to completing the sale."

Howard Putnam
Former CEO, Southwest Airlines
Author of *The Winds of Turbulence*

"Don Hutson's content on how to sell value rather than cut price is legendary. This is a book that WILL make a difference in your sales results. Study it, learn the skills, apply them and your career will never be the same!"

Brad Lea, CEO
Lightspeed VT

Selling Value

Key Principles

— of —

Value-Based Selling

Don Hutson

Dedication

To all sales professionals who are dedicated to learning, for all the good that you do.

Selling Value

Published by:
Executive Books, an imprint of
Tremendous Life Books
118 West Allen Street
Mechanicsburg, PA 17055

717-766-9499   800-233-2665
Fax: 717-766-6565

www.TremendousLifeBooks.com

Paperback ISBN: 978-1-936354-44-3

Hardcover ISBN: 978-0-692-25912-2

Other Works
by the Author

DON HUTSON BOOKS

The Sale

Insights into Excellence
(with members of The Speakers Roundtable)

The Winning Spirit
(anthology)

Inspiring Others to Win
(anthology)

Speaking Secrets of the Masters
(with members of The Speakers Roundtable)

Time Management is an Oxymoron
(with Maynard Rolston)

The Contented Achiever
(with Dr. George Lucas and Chris Crouch)

Selling with Style
(with Dr. Tony Alessandra and Scott Zimmerman)

Taking Charge: Lessons in Leadership
(anthology)

Conversations on Service and Sales
(anthology)

The One Minute Entrepreneur
(with Dr. Ken Blanchard and Ethan Willis)

The One Minute Negotiator
(with Dr. George Lucas)

VIRTUAL TRAINING PROGRAMS FEATURING DON HUTSON

Sell Value, Not Price

Leading and Managing for Prosperity and Performance
(with Mark Sanborn)

Table of Contents

PART ONE

MASTERING THE HEADGAME

PART II

Your Blueprint for Sales Success

PART III

Understanding Your Customer

PART IV
SECURING AND GROWING THE BUSINESS

Foreword

For years I've been saying that you finally become an adult when you realize life is about what you give rather than what you get. The same is true of great salespeople—they understand that their purpose is to genuinely care about and meet the needs of their customers. When you do that, you automatically build trust and become a valued resource.

In other words, selling is not about you—it's about serving the needs of your customer. But how? In other words, what does "serving the needs of your customer" look like in the real world?

Selling Value answers those questions. From preparing for your presentation to closing your sale, Don's comprehensive book provides all the inspiration, information, and coaching you need to become a sales champion—and at the same time, create true value for your customers.

What do I mean by value? As Don points out, the only definition of value that really matters is the one your prospect provides! Too many sales organizations are so wrapped up in their own definition of what's excellent that they don't listen to the only definition that matters: what the prospect wants and needs. Don's book will teach you how to listen and act on what you hear.

When Don and I wrote The One Minute Entrepreneur, we touched on the importance of getting your ego out of the way and focusing on your customer. The fifteen information-packed chapters of Selling Value dive deeply into the who, when, where, what, and how of putting your customer first. You'll learn everything from how to master your own attitude to how to overcome obstacles with creativity and patience.

So study this book, apply its wisdom, and start serving the world by selling value!

—Ken Blanchard
Co-author of *The One Minute Manager*®
and *Leading at a Higher Level*

Introduction

After close to a half century of selling, I have seen so many changes that it would be impossible to enumerate them. In my sales training activities, I have endeavored to bring the latest and best skills to my clients' sales teams. This book is the culmination of the experience and education I have gained on the topic in a way that will help you grow your market share and your client relationships.

The book will confound many critics of the selling profession. My goal is to stimulate and inform people as to the wealth of opportunity intrinsically provided by the development of a customer-centric selling style. I believe the salesperson today is the "gas and oil" of the free enterprise system, and with the proper spirit and skills, can make the world a better place.

Not all of us are professional salespeople but most of us find ourselves selling at some point in our lives. Some people are dispirited by that thought because they think selling is a bad endeavor. The fact is, every time you open your mouth and make an assertion you want to be believed, convincing, and in many cases helpful. Is that a bad thing? I think not.

Some people will selfishly try to persuade others to do something that harms them. These are not professional salespeople; they are people of marginal integrity trying to take advantage of someone else. Please do not get the groups confused!

In his top selling book *To Sell is Human*, Daniel Pinks said, "Selling has changed more in the past ten years than it did in the previous hundred. Most of what we think we understand about selling is constructed atop a foundation of assumptions that has crumbled."

I concur, and it is incumbent upon all of us, if we want to be successful, convincing, and a resource to others, that we gain clarity of thought, visions, goals and actions about how we do business with others. I have written this book to help you do that.

The easiest thing to do today is that which we did yesterday. I implore you to reach out to internalize new skills and hone an ever-improving selling style. Read a minimum of six new books a year on selling. Try new things as you tweak and fine-tune your sales process. Don't procrastinate in embracing technology that can help you be your best. There are many great tools that will enable you to be a more valuable resource to your clients if you will use them.

Okay, that's the big picture. Now let's examine the realities of today's marketplace and the requirements to succeed.

Competition is keener than it has ever been. Many of those with weak resolve have moved on to less intense professions. Only the fit and determined have survived, and they want your market share! Ask questions that make your prospect think and say, "That's a fascinating question—I've never thought about it like that before." Our responsibility is to promote honest dialogue and cause our prospects to see us in a different perspective. The era of the salesperson who stops by and says "Need anything today?" is history. The successful sales professionals today not only stimulate their prospect to think, they work diligently to understand what they value, what their problems are, and to envision how they can become a unique and valued resource.

The biggest mistake I see salespeople making in their attempts to sell value today is the failure to understand how a prospect defines value. Most salespeople are pretty good at articulating the "value points" their marketing department provided for them. The problem is that they may not hit the hot button of a given prospect! Of your five top prospects, there is a good bet they all have different definitions of what they value most. It may be meeting a deadline for one, and for another assuring product availability going forward. For others it might be higher than normal quality standards, special terms, or response to a high priority spec that was previously unimportant to them.

Keep in mind that their perception of value is a moving target. It may not be today what it was 60 days ago. A new Senior VP may have mandated a new buying criterion. We only know when we ask great questions and do in-depth research.

Salespeople are often more obsessed with price than prospects are. I've seen some salespeople work harder to sell their boss on a price cut for a prospect than they do to sell their prospect on the current rate card!

Develop a pleasing and compelling sales personality and embrace the needs and agendas of the multiple constituencies you must serve. Don't settle into a comfort zone that squelches your creativity. Complacency is our enemy. Our challenge is to make ourselves indispensable to our customers.

I hope you find this book to be an invigorating and informing treatise on, not only how to sell value, but also how to align your thinking with the principles that matter most in this crowded marketplace.

Don Hutson
CEO, US Learning

On the back cover you were promised a BONUS! I would like for you to have a 7-day complimentary access into my Interactive Virtual Sales Training Program. For your link into the SELL VALUE, NOT PRICE! system see the "About Author's Services" section in the back of the book on page 312. I hope you enjoy the experience!

PART I

MASTERING THE HEAD GAME

CHAPTER ONE

The Mental Profile
of a Sales Champion

"One cannot directly choose his circumstances, but he can choose his thoughts and indirectly, yet surely, shape his circumstances."

James Allen

ATTITUDE MAKES THE DIFFERENCE

Congratulations for embarking on this learning experience. You have demonstrated that you have an attitude that is receptive to the improvement process, and that's huge—you are in the minority! We all experience a nice bump in self-esteem when we learn new skills that work. A person with high self-esteem naturally seeks the inspiration that comes with learning and growing through such skills as Selling Value, Goal Setting, and the many others we'll cover. I'm convinced this book will help you stretch, grow, and earn more, and I am delighted you have joined us in this experience. My promise is, if you immerse yourself in this content, and learn the skills, more success and prosperity are on the way.

The premise of this chapter is relatively simple but profoundly important. Important enough that it is often the difference between success and failure, or even modest success as compared to magnificent success. Here it is: The attitude you project to others during the sales process influences the response you get, and that attitude is your responsibility, your challenge and your choice. I want you to see this as an opportunity to be seized, not just a task to be accomplished.

The first principle I would ask you to buy into is that attitude is a decision you make many times a day – it is entirely up to you how you handle it. It can be your biggest burden or your greatest opportunity! Every day our attitude is based on the mental programming we individually subscribe to. It is our job to present ourselves in the best way possible.

WHAT YOU SEE IS WHAT YOU GET

Dr. Norman Vincent Peale, the late author of *The Power of Positive Thinking*, told me over dinner one night years ago in Calgary: "Don, I have spent half my life trying to convince people that if they will just think positively and nurture positive expectations that they WILL get more positive results!" He was totally convincing, and his life's work validated his philosophy.

In sales and in life, there is an axiom known as "The Law of the Self-Fulfilling Prophecy." One application of it might well have been on the first page of the first sales book you ever read which goes like this: "Whether you think you are going to make a sale or you think you're not, you are usually right!" Is the power of our own expectations that critical to our success? I'm convinced the answer is an unequivocal yes.

Your attitude will normally be perceived in one of three ways: positive, negative, or apathetic. Great salespeople display an optimistic, hopeful, positive attitude about life and the solutions they are presenting. If you don't believe in your products and solutions, believe me, your prospect won't either.

Do you know what causes salespeople to fail? I spearheaded a survey for Sales and Marketing Executives International, while on their board of directors, in an effort to find out what caused salespeople to fail. The first two items on the list that we learned from our exhaustive search for the answers were very illuminating: The number one failure factor of salespeople was that they failed to properly organize their time and/or their efforts – more on that in a later chapter. It's the second factor that got my attention: The number two failure factor of salespeople is that they negatively, unjustifiably, prejudge the quality of a prospect or the outcome of a sales call. The implication is that many of us shoot ourselves in the foot with a weak attitude or negative expectations, then limp in to make the half-hearted sales call. Let's be sure we NEVER negatively prejudge—give it your best shot every time.

Success in selling is dependent upon having several different critical skill sets, but the foundation of a successful sales career begins with an optimistic attitude. With it, you have a great shot at success; without it you are trying to build a career on an unstable foundation. Remember, it's rare to see whiners winning, or winners whining, in sales organizations today. This is the reason the "Head Game" is so critical to our success.

Greet others with a positive opening. Focus on possibilities and the potential of your business relationship with them as your foundation for success. It was once said that success can only occur when opportunity and preparation meet. I concur. And part of our preparation for achieving great success in selling is to create a mental framework that will position each of us for exceptional results. Without a strong "head game", we are building our career on a shaky foundation.

THE ADVANTAGES OF OPTIMISM

It is my hope that you have now accepted the fact that you make your own decision on the attitudes you possess. Study the subject and make conscious decisions that are in your own enlightened self-interest, and you will be positioning yourself for a life of higher achievement. Much research has indicated that optimistic thinkers achieve more, do better in school, and enjoy more career-related successes than their pessimistic counterparts. Pessimists tend to display a shallower belief in themselves, with lower levels of confidence, and tend to get depressed more often.

In his excellent book *The Optimism Advantage*, Dr. Terry Paulson talks about the practicality of turning your attitudes and actions into positive results. He says that a decision to be an optimist results in you being your own best supporter, while pessimism will result in you being your own worst enemy.

It is really easy to adopt the victim mentality today. Things go wrong many times a day and the easiest thing to do is blame others, get defensive, and go into "poor me" mode. A disciplined optimist refuses to succumb to the temptation to go negative. They know that the positive thinkers tend to get more positive results and they persist in making possibilities become realities. Paulson says the choice is yours. You can trade in your victim mentality and learned helplessness for the optimistic attitudes and actions that will help you develop your own brand of resilience and resourcefulness.

Dr. Martin Seligman, the former president of the American Psychological Association, has challenged psychologists to focus more on positive psychology. In his best-selling book *Learned Optimism*, he asserts that, "Pessimists believe that all misfortunes are their fault, are enduring, and will undermine everything they do." That kind of thinking would do anyone in. The way we think about things can actually diminish or enlarge controls and outcomes. I've never seen a great sales professional who was a devout pessimist. The greats have made the choice for a positive mindset and are largely busy enjoying the fruits of their decision.

Seligman further suggests that, "Our workplace and schools operate on the conventional assumption that success results from a combination of talent and desire. When failure occurs, it is because either talent or desire is missing." His thesis is that when you factor in optimism, better outcomes are on the way.

The famous trial lawyer Edward Bennett Williams was once asked by an interviewer, "Are you a pessimist?" He said, "Of course I'm a pessimist; I'm smart."

I don't buy the assumption that smart people are necessarily negative thinkers. If anything, I believe the reverse is true. Smart individuals have the capacity to consider positive outcomes and possibilities, and strategies to make good things happen. If someone chooses to be a pessimist, it is his own sad fault.

The premise I subscribe to is that attitude is a personal decision that we must make several times a day, and that attitudes do indeed determine outcomes. Remember the words of *Good to Great* author Jim Collins, "You must maintain unwavering faith that you can and will prevail in the end, regardless of the difficulties—and at the same time, have the discipline to confront the most brutal facts of your current reality, whatever it might be."

NICE RIDE!

Don't ever negatively prejudge the result of a sales encounter. On a Saturday morning in Indianapolis, two Rolls-Royce salespeople were standing on the showroom floor talking. An old fellow walked in wearing dirty coveralls with a couple of holes in the knees. He walked over and looked at the Rolls Royce in the showroom, and the salesperson who was up to talk to the next customer thought, what a waste of time, so he blew him off.

So the other salesperson walked over and welcomed him to the dealership. He was courteous and accommodating to him. He subscribed to the philosophy of never, ever prejudging anybody. You don't prejudge them by how they dress; you don't prejudge them by your initial impression. It worked out for this salesman because Mr. Lilly of Eli Lilly Pharmaceuticals bought two Rolls-Royces that morning. One was for himself and one was for his wife. He then went back home and finished his yard work. Don't ever negatively prejudge. If you are going to do any prejudging, positively prejudge.

Is the projection of a balanced, positive demeanor something others have learned to expect of you? If so, that's good. It demonstrates that you have cultivated a very positive habit. Confucius said, "He who cannot smile should not keep shop." I say, "He who does not smile often does not sell often." In selling any product, service, or idea, your disposition will have an impact on the response to your proposition.

REFLEXIVE RESPONSES

When someone asks you, "How are you?" or "How's it going?" what do you say? Most people never stop to think about the impact their answer to that simple question will have. An optimistic answer, accompanied by a pleasant smile, not only helps you build rapport quicker, it also makes you more of a pleasure to do talk to. No one wants to have to carry a pessimistic burden on their shoulders. Be a carrier of sunshine, not sadness.

The mental attitude you display to others becomes much like an invisible magnet which sets the stage for your interaction. It can pull you up to the heights of high achievers who expect good things from life, or it can pull you down among the groveling pessimists.

If we're to get positive results, we must say and do things that contribute to the kind of positive environment that is conducive to successful selling. Another vital reason for a positive response to this simple question is that you are not only setting the stage for the interaction, you are participating in positive self-talk that can intensify your conviction.

THREE CATEGORIES OF MENTAL PROFILE

Let's take a look at three basic categories of mental profile and see if you recognize yourself among them.

In the first category, we find the blind optimist. You've met the blind optimist before. That's the salesperson who is so high and ebullient that you wonder when and if they will ever come in for a landing. This individual is so overwhelmingly optimistic that he or she has difficulty handling problems and routine negative events when they occur.

Don't get me wrong. I really appreciate an individual with a wholesome attitude and an optimistic demeanor. The problem with blind optimists is that their brand of optimism is loud and shallow. When the blind optimist meets with rejection, very often they don't just come in for a landing—they crash!

In earlier years, I was a blind optimist in some ways. For 10 years, I pursued the fun and rewarding hobby of collecting classic and antique cars. I secured some from other collections, but I often purchased these collectibles at classic car auctions throughout the United States. During this chapter in my life, I made an amusing discovery: A blindly optimistic participant in a classic car auction can get his financial knees knocked out from under him in short order. I learned the hard way the subtle and discreet clues to look for in evaluating a car. What you see is not always what you get. I paid handsomely for this learning experience.

While high-performance salespeople project a positive demeanor, they aren't blind optimists. Top pros know that no matter how hard they try and how well prepared they are, they are not going to make a sale every time. This fact is simply a reality of the marketplace. Top pros seem to be mentally prepared for any eventuality.

The high performer may miss one sale, but then he goes on and makes three more sales that day to make up for the one that got away. The blind optimist may be so overwhelmed by one "No" that he or she simply can't get going again. This is non-productive, peak-and-valley behavior. Don't allow yourself to be so optimistic that you are emotionally ill-equipped to deal with reality, which invariably deals us rejection, periodic discontent and unavoidable problems along with the joy we are entitled to.

In the second category of mental profiles we find the reality optimist. This is the category in which most high performance sales professionals are found.

Reality optimists think rationally when they go out into the marketplace. They say to themselves, "My conversion rate has been X lately. Now I'm going to try to reach 100 percent, but after I've given it my best shot, if I don't make a sale, I'm not going to let that ruin my day."

As a salesperson, you can listen to CDs, watch DVDs and instructional videos, you can read books, you can pick the brains of your sales manager—all these things are good and can help you improve your conversion rate. While these factors can have an impact on it, you can never control the behavior of your prospective clients. When a client declines to buy, the reality optimist says to himself, "Okay, I'll get the sale next time!" and then goes right on to the next client. You may not be in control of a client's decision, but you can be in control of how you will let rejection affect your attitude.

I have never met a high performance professional who did not have belief and optimism. These individuals are well balanced and organized, so that when they do experience rejection, it's like water off a duck's back. The blind optimist, by contrast, sets himself or herself up for failure due to an inability to handle negative events of the marketplace.

In the third category of mental profile we find the pessimist. This is the person who cheers everyone up when he leaves the room.

Once a salesman and sales manager were making calls. The manager said, "Hey, that looks like a great prospect over there! We've never called on that company. Let's make a cold call on them right now."

The pessimistic salesman said, "Might as well skip it. They're lousy prospects. I haven't called on them, but I've heard about them. They're not going to buy anything from us."

The sales manager came unglued. He said, "What kind of attitude is that? If you're going to be successful in the profession of selling, you've got to be positive!"

The salesman replied, "OK boss, I'm positive they ain't gonna buy anything from us!"

Given the choice, I can't imagine why anyone would prefer to think negatively, but many do. Negative thinking is usually a carelessly acquired bad habit rather than a well-thought-out decision. Instead, vigorously nurture the habit of reality optimism.

The pessimist stacks the cards against himself. The reality optimist not only stacks the cards in his favor; some would say he controls the game.

OUTLOOK AFFECTS OUTCOMES

Our thinking processes control much of our life, and the image we have of ourselves certainly affects our sales performance. My favorite author and literary mentor Orison Swett Marden said, "A one-talent person with an overmastering self-faith often accomplishes infinitely more than a ten-talent person who does not believe in himself."

A study conducted several years ago by the University of Chicago supports the theory that your outlook can actually affect your life. The study even revealed that people who are ill but don't think of themselves as sick often enjoy a better healthier life than people who are not sick but believe they are.

What causes people to be negative and pessimistic anyway? Pessimistic people experience what they perceive as a negative event or situation and they choose to become depressed. Perhaps it's a subconscious choice, but that's the result—depression. We are born to win but sometimes self-conditioned to lose.

We also attract what we think. Negative thoughts produce negative results. On the other hand, positive thoughts are the basis for successful attitudes and successful habits, habits that lead directly to positive results in everything we do.

High performance salespeople realize the importance of keeping a positive, realistic, wholesome frame of reference. They know that positive expectations lead to positive results.

The image and attitude you project are largely developed by habit. If you have the habit of projecting negative thoughts and feelings, reevaluate your behavior and make a conscious effort to change. The payoff could be great.

Remember that fear, doubt, and continuous procrastination are symptoms of the disease called lack of confidence, and lack of confidence is nurtured by negative thinking and the absence of an action plan. In the words of the philosopher William James, "It is our attitude at the beginning of a difficult undertaking which, more than anything else, will determine its successful outcome."

The pessimist sees the problems in each opportunity, while the optimist sees the opportunities in each problem. High performance salespeople see themselves as professional problem-solvers. They capitalize on each opportunity with a positive belief in the results they can gain and the people they can help.

If you want to succeed in selling, choose to vigorously nurture the habit of reality optimism. That choice will be a big step in the direction of higher sales performance and greater prosperity.

My friend Randy Jones, the former president of a medical firm, shared this interesting story with me.

Shortly after acquiring Deseret Medical, our sales management team at Warner Lambert Corporation was faced with a dangerous morale slump. Old-line salespeople began grumbling about having been "taken over" by a large corporation and having lost the free-spirited, entrepreneurial atmosphere that had made their company a sales-driven success in the past. They were afraid that their skills and individuality would be buried in the quagmire of corporate structure.

I was president of the management unit for sales and was faced with the task of keeping our sales force positive in the midst of the massive changes that they considered threatening. Complaints ran a wide gamut, from new report forms and procedures to different designs for business cards. The declining situation boiled over when another new policy mandating smaller company cars was introduced, driving the field sales force into a frenzy. Our management staff listened closely to the sales representatives, then devised a program that we hoped would turn negatives into positives. We felt we had come up with a winner.

We introduced a special six-month sales contest in which each of the top 10 sales achievers in our 96-person sales team would receive a Mercedes Benz on a two-year lease as their company car. Result? An immediate turnaround in morale and a 15 percent increase in average per-person sales productivity! We no longer heard complaints about company cars, since such comments would naturally yield a discussion on performance—i.e., get into the top 10 and earn yourself a real prestige company car!

Everyone had a shot at this great incentive program, and it worked. We simply impacted a negative situation with a positive program. The sales force recognized that management was neither too stilted nor too stuffy to have a little fun and that maybe things could actually get better than during "the good old days".

THREE WAYS TO DISPLAY A POSITIVE SELF-IMAGE

Henry David Thoreau once said, "If one advances confidently in the direction of his own dreams and endeavors to live the life which he has imagined, he will meet with a success unexpected in common hours." Our self-image accompanied by positive expectations can take us to new levels.

First let's define the term "present self-image." Your present self-image is your perception of your strengths and your weaknesses at this time. It is a snapshot of yourself in the here and now.

The most powerful force you possess is what you say to yourself and truly believe. Positive self-talk not only enhances your present self-image. I'm convinced it also expands your productive capacity. It programs you for more action and results.

I hope your present self-image is always improving, because it's consistent with the growth process. The image you have had of yourself in the past has delivered you to where you are today, and your self-image each day in the future will take you to where you are going to be.

Charisma transplants and success implants still aren't available, so we must look for other avenues to enhance our self-image and how we display it to others. Here are three excellent ways you can help yourself build a strong self-image:

ONE: WRITE DOWN
YOUR PERSONAL POSITIVE AFFIRMATIONS

Examples of career-related positive affirmations for professional sales-people might be "I am performing my needs analysis better each time I do it" or "I am eagerly and successfully focusing on customer needs better than ever." For best results, keep them in the present tense.

Positive affirmations help you feel better about yourself at present, and they pave the way for growth and progress in the future. Frequently reviewed positive affirmations, whether personal or professional, tend to enhance what you expect and get from yourself. Remember this maxim: "Whatever the mind of man can conceive and believe, it can achieve."

TWO: CONSTANTLY ANALYZE AND
ADDRESS YOUR STRENGTHS AND WEAKNESSES

Self-assessment is extremely valuable, especially when we also get input from others whose opinions we respect. Successful people identify their human strengths and build on those strengths as their foundation for success. Simultaneously, they identify their personal weaknesses, eliminating as many weaknesses as they can and at least managing those weaknesses that can't be easily eliminated.

Your plan of action for a better life should be built on the foundation of your strengths. Remember, however, that you should never make someone else's opinion of you more important than your opinion of yourself.

During a recent National Speakers Association address, motivational speaker Les Brown said, "If greatness is possible, then good intentions, good follow-through, even periodic excellence are insufficient. Be a no-limit thinker! When we don't know what the limits are, we assume we don't have any, and that increases the chance that we will perform with greatness."

We must diligently and constantly pursue personal excellence. Sometimes significant behavior changes are in order, but in many instances if you feel good about yourself, only minor changes may be needed to get you to where you truly want to be.

What level of success do you currently see for yourself? I once heard a successful general agent of one of the major life insurance companies tell his agents this: "The income level you expect to enjoy should be reflected by the income level of the clients you comfortably converse with." I guess that was his way of asking, "Are you a $40,000 salesperson talking to $40,000 clients, or are you a $200,000 salesperson talking to $200,000 clients?"

Your self-image will determine your level of expectations. Mutt Easley, a buddy in high school, told me he was sure he'd never get married. When I asked why, he said, "Because any woman who would marry me isn't good enough for me." The guy needed to work on his self-image.

Walt Disney said, "The more you are like yourself, the less you are like anyone else, thus approaching uniqueness." Embrace your own individuality. Be yourself, be proud of who and what you are, but never usurp your opportunities to grow.

THREE: HAVE A STRONG VISION TO REACH TOWARD

What is the rest of your life going to be like? Do you believe you are either destined to succeed or destined to fail in your life? What you visualize is what you will attract.

I submit that your future will be more of a decision than a destiny. Your present thoughts and plans will largely determine your future. And since you control your thoughts and your plans, you control your own future.

"Projected self-image" is the phrase I use to refer to your vision of yourself in the future. Your projected self-image is comprised of your strengths, your weaknesses, your levels of success and attainment as you imagine them to be at some future point. Intense, detailed visualization is required to program the subconscious mind for a better life and higher sales production.

The power of the human visualization process is truly awesome. Once you program your conscious mind with definitive data from that powerful imagination, your subconscious mind goes to work to make it happen.

Just remember, though, that if the conscious mind never gets the data, it cannot be passed along to the subconscious mind for action. Let's return to my premise that your future as a high performance salesperson is more of a decision than a simple destiny. What can you do to make the right decisions that will result in the vision, then the reality, of high performance? Set your thermostat!

It may sound like an over-simplification, but programming your subconscious mind is almost as simple as setting the thermostat in your home. You can turn it up or turn it down, but don't ever fool yourself into thinking that you haven't set it. Most people have their thermostats set far too low. They may have let the negative influence of other people psyche them out. Many will go to their graves with their music still in them because they never turned up their expectation and achievement thermostat.

One of my most gratifying moments as a speaker came when I was addressing Healthco International. Following my three-hour sales and personal development seminar, Regional Manager Gerry Mundy got up and said to his sales force, "After hearing this program, I'm convinced our $93 million annual goal is too low. Should we go for $100 million?" The salespeople cheered and responded resoundingly, so they raised their goal. I learned later that they hit it. What would you attempt if you were confident you couldn't miss your goal?

THE BIRD'S-EYE VIEW: DREAMS ABOUNDING

Don't have a bug's eye view of the future. Have a bird's eye view. See the bigger picture. Think of the people you can help, the lives you can positively touch, the joys you can share with others. What potential do we have when we envision possibilities? Those with the bugs-eye view have very limited visibility – those piles of carpet the bug crawls through are thick! The people with the birds-eye view have few limits!

A well-considered projected self-image will be the thermostat by which you set your achievement level and ultimately your lifestyle. Too many people allow others to set their thermostats. Don't do it. This is no dress rehearsal. Today is the real deal.

Life itself is usually a self-fulfilling prophecy. You can make it work to your benefit rather than to your detriment. I agree with Gregory Baum who said, "Every person is called upon to create his future." Unleash your imagination, focus on a noble vision, and go for it!

Most failures use up as much energy failing as successful people do succeeding. Plan your success with a vengeance. Remember, you are probably not as good today as you are going to be someday. Accelerate your achievement rate now. There is no reason to wait!

MOTIVATION TO THE MAX!

High performers are motivated and ready to make great things happen! If they get some motivation from their boss or significant other, or another source, that's fine, but they understand that their PRIMARY source of motivation comes from within. Yes, in its purest form, all motivation is self-motivation. Someone cannot be motivated who mentally refuses to be motivated, unless it is through basic fear for their life or safety, and we don't see that customarily in the workplace. Let's work to understand the definition and philosophy of motivation for salespeople, but also the applications we need to have in place to excel.

The model that has worked well for us in our training activities assumes there are two dimensions to the motivational process. One is direction, which will be either positive or negative, depending on what one says and does. The other is intensity, which will be either high, with positive energy to achieve, or low, with deficient energy to do well.

This will give us four potential variables: First is positive direction and high intensity, which is where we want to be. It means you will be saying and doing the right things, and doing a lot of it! Secondly, we have positive direction but low intensity, which means results will be compromised somewhat; third, we have negative direction and low intensity which means we are doing the wrong things and not even doing much of that. And last we have negative direction and high intensity—which is really scary. We are doing the wrong things, and doing lots of it. Immediate behavior modification is in order in that case. So let's do our best on every aspect of our sales career—think quality and quantity.

Zig Ziglar had a great quote: "You can get anything you want in life if you just help enough other people get what they want!" Yes, sales success is the humility to help others, not just the ego to win. As we are motivated to zero in on each prospective customer's specific needs and an understanding of what they value, we are positioning ourselves to be of great value to them.

BE A CHAMPION OF CHANGE

I'll bet you have heard the cliché that "If you keep on doing what you have been doing, you will keep on getting what you have always gotten!" I believe that axiom used to be true, but not anymore. Things are changing too rapidly.

The "bar of excellence" is moving up on every one of us every day. Competition is getting keener. Buyers are smarter and more demanding. And we won't be able to take allegiance for granted. In today's marketplace we need to be able to turn-on-a-dime to please customers. And that means we can't be married to the processes and habits of the past.

The experts on change today are saying that the knowledge mass of the human race is now doubling approximately every four years. So, yes, the one constant we can be assured of is CHANGE. What is your change quotient? Do you have a good spirit about change and find ways to make change work for you, or do you feel threatened by change and the new requirements thrust upon you to excel in an ever challenging environment?

My colleague and friend, industrial psychologist Dr. Paul Green, says one key metric people consider today in hiring new talent is their "tolerance for ambiguity." How do you deal with the unexpected? It has been said that most people change when the pain NOT to change exceeds the pain to change! I suggest you broaden your perspective, see the big picture when talking with prospects, and be willing to change and adapt to succeed.

We might as well decide right now to be optimistic and find ways to buy-in to the changes that come our way, unless, of course, we can impact the precipitating event to make it work better for us or others. Most changes are beyond our control, so I vote for finding the possibilities within them.

Legendary business consultant Dr. Peter Drucker once said that "one sign of incompetence and resulting ineffectiveness is when one constantly focuses on their successes of the past." Did you ever know anyone who always talked about "the good old days" as if they were the only days to talk about? These people need to get in the present and engage with today's reality.

High performers identify problems of clients, often before the client even articulates them. They envision solutions for a client before anyone has thought of it. They develop the attitude and capability to 'turn on a dime' to help a client solve a problem.

> To be a valued resource to your prospects and clients, be solution oriented and think about possibilities for them, not just the same old tired answers people in your industry have been putting on the table for years. Be the architect of positive circumstance, not the victim of negative happenstance. Those who wish to sing always find a song.

Priceless

CHAPTER TWO

Minimizing Rejection and Maximizing Performance

"If a salesperson does not know statistically and productively exactly where he has been, it will be impossible to intelligently and accurately project where he is going."

DICK GARDNER

In our continuing quest to master the "head game" in selling, we need to know our track record. To confidently go into the marketplace and sell the value of our offering, we need to have our act together in all regards. The numbers game, once mastered by sales professionals, will inspire them to improve in every respect that is measured.

Our ultimate success in selling is determined by the number of contacts we make and how good we are when we deal with them. The highest performers seem to be able to find the means and methods of compressing more achievement into a given measurable time frame than other salespeople. Occasionally, obstacles slow us down or get us off track. These are the times that separate the cream of the crop from the rest of the field. We need the discipline not to be knocked off track and to execute the plan for the day. The recommendation is to simultaneously work to improve our skill sets and our understanding of the latest and best sales ideas to excel in today's market.

This skill is challenging to learn and internalize but disastrous to ignore. High performance salespeople need to understand the essence of their numbers in every aspect of their sales activities. They know that nobody makes a sale every time. I'm sure you've noticed this common fact of selling. A lot of people say "No".

NOBODY SELLS EVERYBODY

One of the most glaring reasons people fail in the sales profession is their inability to handle rejection. They take it personally, become demoralized, and their "head game" is trashed and out of sorts. So psychologically dealing with the unpleasantness of rejection becomes very important in one's framework of thinking. Nobody sells everybody. Not even the best of the best. Nobody is that good. But may I also suggest that there is no salesperson who can miss everybody either. Nobody is that bad, especially when you have a great, high-value product. Somebody could fumble all over themselves and still sell a great product from time to time. You know the blind hog line, right? Even he can find an acorn once in a while.

I don't know what your conversion rate is, but I hope you know. What percentage of your prospects do you convert to confirmed sales? Get a handle on this and other key numbers, and then never let your guard down. Keeping up with your numbers can have a tremendous impact on your level of sales excellence. Once you know your numbers you can work to increase that percentage from 21 to 30 percent or from 71 to 75 percent. When you know your numbers you focus on them and your subconscious mind goes to work to help you improve them.

One day while conducting a training session, I made the statement that nobody can sell everybody. A man in the back of the room stood up and interrupted me. He said, "I beg to differ with you, Don. I want you to know that I sell everybody I talk to!"

I thought I misunderstood him. So I walked back and I said, "Pardon me. I'm not sure I understood you correctly." And again he said, "I sell everybody I talk to. I never miss."

I said, "Obviously you aren't making enough calls!"

The audience roared. Here was a guy who probably made two calls a month for two months and got lucky four times. Big producers have bigger numbers, and some rejection is always part of their success formula. The fact is, winners know that periodically losing is an integral part of the success process.

It's easy once in a while to lean back and rely 100 percent on provided leads or established accounts rather than doing any creative prospecting. It's easy to let our guard down. The numbers game can be a powerful force for personal growth and motivation. The salesperson who doesn't understand percentages will be utterly discouraged when the door doesn't open for him or her. But a mature salesperson will realize that when a door doesn't open, he or she is still better off than before the call because they are statistically that much closer to a yes. For most salespeople aggressive prospecting and new account acquisition is a key part of the mix for success, so keep filling your "pipeline" with new prospects.

Rejection, and your response to it, is very much a part of sales success. Without it, you will never get to the yeses. With it, your process will work. Rejection is simply a valuable form of feedback. As Ken Blanchard says "Feedback is the breakfast of champions!"

UNDERSTANDING THE NUMBERS GAME

To fully understand this philosophy, let's consider an example. The figures I use here may not fit your selling situation perfectly, but for the sake of simplicity, let's go with them.

Assume that your averages are such that you have to make ten calls to talk to four people. After you talk to four prospects, do your needs analysis, and give four presentations, you confirm one sale, and your average income is $1,000 per sale. That means, in hard numbers, that each presentation earned you $250, even if they said "No." And each call made you $100, even if they wouldn't listen to you.

Sound absurd? It's not—it's the numbers game. If you accept this basic philosophy, you will understand that ultimately you must maximize contact with people who can say "Yes" and be effective when you do. This rational reflection of simple numbers will philosophically serve you very well, because you will never again feel that your success or failure as a professional salesperson is on the line with any one prospect. An understanding of this principle will also keep most of the negative emotion out of your sales activities. Yes, you must go through the nos to earn the right to experience the yeses.

High performers have a special ability to fail successfully. They learn from experience and have no negative hang-ups that their image has been tarnished. They're already too busy on their next achievement to allow these destructive thoughts to enter their minds.

Another aspect of the numbers game is to continually analyze your personal sales cycles. Your sales cycle is defined as the length of time which transpires from the first time you converse with a prospect until you get an order from him or her. It is a simple measurement of time, but when you keep up with your cycle times, you will find yourself thinking about it, focusing on it, improving it, and earning more in the process.

High performance salespeople are students of their own sales cycles. These pros are always evaluating their sales process, trying to figure out how they can build trust more proficiently so they can secure orders more quickly. The sales cycle numbers they endlessly evaluate pertain to such vital statistics as number of contacts during a given time frame, number of days in the sales cycle, average length of a sales cycle during a three or six-month period, average income per sale, and percentage of customers who buy repeatedly versus one-time buyers.

YOUR BEST SHOT ON EVERY CALL

Because high performance salespeople know their numbers, they are keenly aware of their own track record. This enables them to not be bothered by a periodic no. If you ever reach a point in your career when you hang your feelings of self-worth on one call or one customer, you're on the way out.

Successful salespeople realize that one who gives a half-hearted presentation because he or she is talking to what's perceived as only a "fair" prospect is shooting himself or herself in the foot. The empirical data is in and it supports the premise that extraordinary presentations delivered by salespeople with above-average levels of belief in the value of their offering, sincerity and enthusiasm can and often convert "fair" prospects into buyers. Pros give it their best shot in every interaction with every prospect every time!

Does playing the numbers game and keeping score in your sales career seem too unimportant to fool with? Have you rationalized the cliché you heard years ago that good salespeople are lousy on detail? If so, you are playing an old tape and need to erase it or throw it away.

Keep score. Know your numbers. Don't fall prey to the belief that business is good or bad because of circumstances beyond your control. Buy into the idea that business is good or bad when you make it so.

Just as a skilled pilot would not consider taking off without consulting his checklist, don't try to succeed without having your numbers down cold. If you don't know your numbers, you will ultimately work for less income per hour and per day, and you'll experience much more stress and frustration. And it will be much harder to give it your best on every call.

DEALING SUCCESSFULLY WITH REJECTION

When you lose a sale, get over it fast. All salespeople experience it, but the pros move on to the next encounter with a positive attitude, realizing that they are statistically that much closer to getting a yes.

Here are eight tips for effectively dealing with rejection with the minimum amount of mental anguish:

1. Don't take rejection personally. It's not about you. It is simply part of the sales process.

2. Give every call and presentation your best effort. It is only through constant improvement that we can enjoy better statistics.

3. Keep up with your numbers with a vengeance, so that you always know exactly what is required to succeed.

4. Know that you begin to succeed when you learn how to fail, and sort out the implications of how failure is a part of your success plan.

5. The greater your expectations, the greater your determination to succeed.

6. Understand that we grow stronger when we experience adversity.

7. Even when you are rejected, you can learn from it.

8. Remember that you never lose until you give up. On another day you may sell them; they might even become your biggest account someday. Don't burn any bridges.

IF YOU'RE DOWN, GET UP (AND KEEP SCORE!)

If you ever find yourself in another slump, you have to make a choice. You can wallow slovenly in a sea of self-pity, or you can turn on your afterburner and make something happen.

Here's my basic formula for getting out of a slump:

1. Identify the degree to which your business is off. (Example: down 21 percent from this time last month or last quarter)

2. Identify the three or four things that have contributed the most to your success, uniqueness and performance in the past.

3. Develop a plan to immediately get in contact with 21 percent more people than you've been calling on thus far this month or quarter.

4. When making those contacts, concentrate on the positive behaviors and techniques that you identified in Number Two above.

5. Evaluate your existing customer base for additional potential sales, either more volume in like items or the sale of additional products.

Simple? Yes. Does it work? You bet! Try it and I predict you will see immediate improvement. As Orison Swett Marden said, "The stream of plenty will not flow toward stingy, parsimonious, doubting thought. Wealth must be created mentally first."

KNOW YOUR NUMBERS AND FILL THE PIPELINE

In your effort to maximize your sales performance, you must do your research and homework. When you make prospecting calls, know exactly how many are required to reach your goals. Know at all times the number of Needs Analyses you've performed and have in progress, and the number of sales confirmed within a given time frame. Until and unless you know your numbers, you will never be able to set goals with a credible procedure or function with maximum confidence.

Remember the pipeline concept. If we know our numbers, and we continue to fill the pipeline (make new calls), good things happen. Sales will result over a given period of time. Theoretically, once your pipeline is full every time you make a call results will come out the other end. It's foolproof.

If you know your numbers and give a high-quality presentation every time, you will never be at the mercy of momentary emotion during your career. You'll know what must be done for your next piece of business to come together. Even if you know you are presenting to an 'only fair' prospect, what if they don't buy but give you the referral of a lifetime?! If any presentation is worth giving, it is worth giving well.

Most salespeople who have "emotional highs" that they capitalize on also have "emotional lows" that they suffer from. Understanding and practicing the Numbers Game can take the emotional lows out of the picture without destroying our emotional highs.

CLEAR RESULTS FROM CLEAR OBJECTIVES

If we are not careful, we will get casual about our process of making calls, and that can cause casualties in our performance. ALWAYS have a clear call objective when making a call. Even better, write it down and program yourself for positive results that are specific in nature. When you have a carefully defined call objective better things happen on your calls. Perhaps it is simple like "Since I haven't talked to Dale in three months I need to re-establish rapport and update her on our latest new product development discoveries." Or "The biggest need for this sales call is to get Terry to provide the names and titles of the other three people who are in the decision loop, and get his blessings on me talking to them."

We can learn from this story told by Jerry Anzalone, general sales manager for Sylvan Pools in Phoenix, Arizona. There are more swimming pools per capita in Phoenix than anywhere in the world. But there are also more than 100 companies in the business, so successful operators have to be optimistic and never prejudge prospects, as Jerry explains.

I was in the office late one afternoon doing some paperwork. It was about 5:30, and everyone had gone but me and one salesman, whose name was John. He was new on our team and still learning how to sell.

A call came in from a woman who wanted to know if someone could come by her house that evening and talk to her about buying a pool. John's schedule was clear so I sent him out to make the call. But when he found out the woman lived in South Phoenix, his face fell.

"Those people down there can't pass for credit," John said. "They're low income. They can't afford swimming pools."

I decided to go on the sales call with John. I closed down the office, and we both got in John's car to drive out to South Phoenix. Even though he was new to sales, John new the pool business fairly well because he had previously owned a company.

We entered the neighborhood where our prospect lived. Graffiti was everywhere, covering walls and fences. The houses were small, most of them were run down, and they all looked a lot alike. But we found the right address. Our knock was answered by an attractive woman in her early 30's. We stepped inside, and it was like entering Shangri La. Neat and beautiful. You could have eaten off the floor.

She made a pitcher of lemonade, and we talked about the design of the pool she wanted. I told her we could give her an estimate to compare with other prices. Her response should have taught John more about negative pre-judging than any lecture I might have prepared.

She wasn't planning to talk to any other company, she said. She had called five other pool companies that day before calling us. As soon as she gave them her name and address, they started backing up. The first two said they would mail credit applications and come out after the credit cleared. The next two said they were too busy and would send someone later. The fifth company said they never came to her area at night.

"You were the only person who responded instantly, without prejudice or reservation," she said. "I felt then that you'd be a good person to work with. Now I'm convinced." We built the exact pool she wanted and she paid cash for it.

We had blitzed the competition and had this sale in the bag, all because we had an open mind and a desire to sell a pool to anybody we could!

Not too long after that day, John left us to go with another pool company. He said the other company provided "better leads." I guess John didn't learn the good lesson that was there for him to learn in South Phoenix. A positive attitude and going for the numbers can help you succeed. It works when you have good leads, and it even works when you don't. You've got to believe you can succeed on every call.

Before every call, I tell myself this: "The best thing that can happen is that I'm going to make this sale! And the worst thing that can happen is that I'm going to get in some very good practice!"

THE HIGH PERFORMANCE SELLING MODEL

U.S. Learning's High Performance Model for sales professionals helps them achieve high performance status. The model has been researched and fine-tuned for some time. It shows the components that make up the high performance behavior we see in the best sales professionals.

The question I have been asked most during my sales training career is "What are the consistently high performing sales professionals doing to keep their status?" While I have always thought it was a great question, for a long time it was difficult to answer. But finally, after years of research, I have figured it out. It is not a short and simple answer, just a very good answer, so stay with me.

First, top salespeople are "up" in terms of their attitude, as we discussed in chapter one. If their attitude is aligned for success their prospects are very good for making headway.

Secondly, top salespeople are "good" in terms of the skill sets learned and utilized on a daily basis. They are constantly studying their craft, reading books, on the Internet, advancing their knowledge of both the products they are selling and the sales skills needed to compete successfully.

In sales we are only as good as our reflex actions! The high performers maintain a desire to continually improve their skills. They are the men and women who practice, drill and rehearse constantly. They are eager to role-play, so that they can internalize sales skills so well that they are available to them as "reflexes" when needed to make sales. There is nothing more frustrating than remembering what you should have said instead of what you did say AFTER losing a sale!

One question I am often asked is "Are the top performers up because they are good, or good because they are up?"

I said "Great question. The answer is YES". Being up in your attitude and good at what you do are both vital attributes which feed on each other, giving salespeople the opportunity to create what I like to call positive momentum. When things are going well they tend to get better, so do what you can to create and sustain positive momentum in your sales efforts.

Let's dig deeper into the high performance model. What does being up look like? I think it means one has identified the elements of his propulsion process. What is it that keeps you excited about your career, and fired up to produce excellent results and keep a positive attitude? It is different things for different people. Here are some potential answers to the question of one's propulsion factor:

- Inspiration from another person

- Attending sales seminars

- Reading the latest sales books released

- Reading older self-help books

- Internet research to learn about clients

- Monetary goals

I don't need to know what your "Propulsion Factor" is, but it is very important that you know, because you will need to tap into it as a source of power quite often. Notice on the next illustration that when we have identified our propulsion factor, we are thrust into better more productive behaviors that increase our performance.

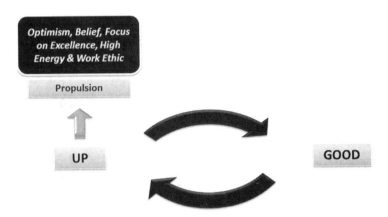

So what happens when someone has not identified or clarified their propulsion factor? It will be very difficult to stay centered on highly productive behavior. When the propulsion factor is not in play, gravity takes over and that can ugly fast. If gravity comes into play one descends into a lack of commitment, and a negative mental profile.

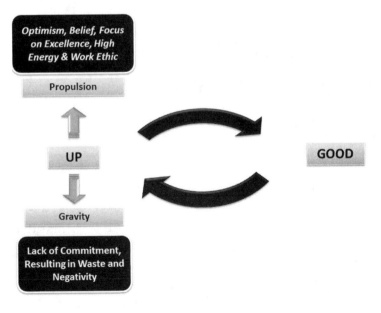

On the other side of the model we see that being highly skilled, or good at what we do, is facilitated by having a hunger for knowledge and desire for new skill sets gained through a solid training initiative. This will result in one having and demonstrating cutting edge skills and innovative solutions.

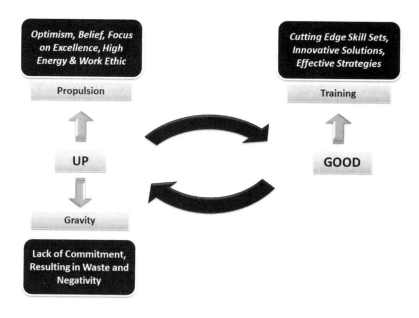

In the absence of a viable source of training and development, one tends to fall back into old habits which results in a complacent spirit and the presentation of tired solutions.

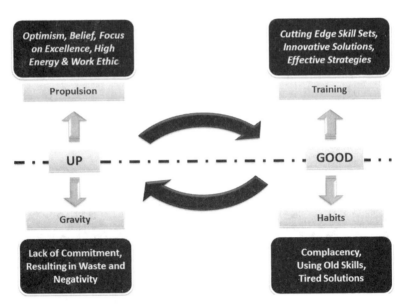

The key is for us to each be vigorous enough in our efforts to stay above the (dotted) average line to be exceptional. Too many sales people today are sixes and think they are nines. If you turn on the "afterburner" and work hard to be both UP and GOOD, it will result in you working harder and smarter and with greater determination to excel than those of your competitors.

Most of those who fail use up as much energy failing as successful people do succeeding. Plan your success with a vengeance. You are not as good today as you will be at some future point in time, so vow to accelerate your achievement process now! There is no reason to wait.

CHAPTER THREE

Internalizing the New Model for Successful Selling

"I've always believed that it's important to show a new look periodically. Predictability can lead to failure."

T. BOONE PICKENS

If you are attempting to sell today the same as you were just five years ago you run the risk of being outrun by your competition. Massive changes have transpired requiring us to do and be much more than in the past and today's buyer is savvy. This book will help you make the transition to a clearly understood path of sales excellence which will delight your prospects and clients, and give you more peace of mind.

The significance of the success we will enjoy will largely be based on the significance of the solutions we provide for our clients. Bill Gates cared more about creating software than he did about being rich. His passion resulted in great wealth, but it was because of the significance of what he created for others.

THE EVOLUTION OF SELLING

If we are going to separate ourselves from the competition in the eyes of our clients, we cannot be just another "me too" salesperson. We need to have a better sales approach. In this chapter we will look at what is working today and what is not, and why.

I'd like to take you through the U.S. Learning model we refer to as "The 5 Stages in The Evolution of Selling." The key today is to develop a "selling style" that customers are comfortable with, or we will be unable to build trust. We need to sell them in a way that increases the probability that they will get engaged with us, talk openly about their issues, opinions, and preferences. If we can get them talking and feeling comfortable with us, we have a great shot at getting an order and establishing a long term relationship.

The first two stages of the evolution of selling are outdated and unacceptable for high integrity selling today. They are presented here for your consideration as a historical perspective only. They are manipulative, unprofessional, and contributed to the negative image of selling that still exists in many people's minds today. Here are the five stages with three descriptors of each stage to further our understanding.

1. The Product Pitch:

    a. A narrow, self-serving approach

    b. No tailored solution, but an attempt sell the masses

    c. Often offering products of little or no value

2. The Hard Sell:

    a. Pressure based

    b. Often "closing" before earning the right

    c. Destroys rather than builds trust

3. Relationship Selling:

    a. A high level of trust is enjoyed by the parties

    b. Relationship stress is kept at a minimum

    c. Adaptability is present among both parties

4. Needs-Analysis Selling:

    a. Information gathering is the cornerstone

    b. The customer's agenda is ever-present

    c. Constant monitoring for pertinent changes

5. Symbiotic Selling:

    a. Allegiance is present in the relationship

b. Eagerness to work together toward common goals

c. Collaboration grows from the symbiotic competencies developed

If we are attempting to sell with the last three approaches we have a good chance of creating a strong following in the marketplace and enjoying high levels of success. Craft a selling style that is respectful of others, focused on their needs, and their definition of value, and you are on your way to a successful selling career.

THE STRESS/TRUST RELATIONSHIP

In business relationships stress and trust are usually inversely proportional. The reason the product pitch and the hard sell don't work anymore is because they defy the logic of trust-building behaviors. When somebody treats you like a member of the masses and expects you to buy their stuff because they gave a slick presentation, or had an answer to each of your objections, they are delusional.

Product pitches and hard sell activities are not conducive to building trust. When you try to get someone to make a decision before earning the right and asking excellent questions, you are usually increasing the interpersonal stress of the prospect. As his stress in dealing with you goes up, his trust in you goes down. As shown in this illustration, the net effect of this is that your behavior has decreased their tendency to buy from you, thus creating poor conversion rates and long sales cycles.

The "Undesirable Model"

THE SALES CYCLE—LESS IS MORE!

As discussed earlier, the sales cycle is the length of time which transpires from the moment of the first interaction with someone about a given product, service or idea, until the affirmative decision is gained. There is a fine line between keeping the sales cycle efficiently short and devoting the necessary time to sales calls and prospect encounters required to build trust and get the order.

The highest producing salespeople have figured out how to compress more achievement into a given measurable time frame without violating the rules of good needs analysis and advanced client engagement. Our success in most endeavors is traditionally measured by how much achievement takes place over a given measurable time frame. Be as efficient in your sales process as possible, while giving your prospects the time and interest required to do an exceptional job for them. The net effect is that you will be selling with considerably higher efficiency. This illustration shows the effect of a high trust sales approach.

The "Desirable Model"

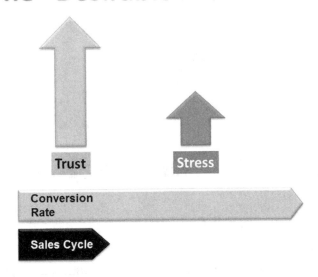

BECOME A VALUE-BASED TRUSTED ADVISOR

Being a "Trusted Advisor" is an honorable position. It means that you are respected as a professional with unique and appreciated talents. These attributes, in the right measure, will often set you apart from your competition. Here are four behavioral components that you find in trusted advisors:

1. Integrity and Character
2. Demonstrated Expertise
3. Timely Follow Through
4. Understand Their Prospect

Most of the folks being called on can tell the difference between a salesperson out to just make a sale rather than build a relationship. One of the biggest mistakes many salespeople make is failing to understand what their prospects and clients really value. One may value a ship date the most, another the best price, and another compliance with his company's terms. It is the salesperson's responsibility to learn what each prospect values most. Do all you can to honestly deliver value by their definition and your just rewards will be forthcoming.

THE ANATOMY OF THE SALES CALL

Legendary speaker, Arthur "Red" Motley, said "Nothing happens until somebody sells something!", and I agree with him to this day. But to expound on this philosophy further, I say that "Today, nobody sells anything until they make a sales call or are fortunate enough to have someone contact them." The more and better the calls we engage in, the greater the level of success we enjoy in sales! This section is all about improving the quality and quantity of our sales calls.

In this critical skill, we will cover the things that matter most in understanding, managing, and executing our sales call process. We will cover it in multiple steps.

First, have a well-organized, viable system of organizing your prospects. The currency of the future is your database! How are you doing in managing and organizing your book of business? How much attention are you paying to who is in your database, how much information you have captured about them, and how accurate is it? Few things are more important, in the overall scheme of things, than your database. Plan your prospecting function so as to have a balance in new calls, follow-up calls, service-related calls and any other types to be certain you are meeting all time lines of importance.

Manage the communications flow with your team members who are in the loop either in making team calls with you or being in the mix on following up items you may have promised. For an efficient process, always be keenly aware of who "OWNS" an issue or project associated with your sales efforts.

Review notes and update all data. You want your calls to go better than those of your competitors! Consider all previous communications you have had with them, and be able to suggest who else from their side you might need to be a part of the appointment. Research everything you can to get to know them better. Visit their website and Google them to learn all you can. Check out Facebook or LinkedIn or other social media outlets for more information that might prove helpful.

There is a trend toward more team selling in the marketplace today, probably due to more subject matter experts being needed to help solve more complex problems. Be diligent in team sales call planning. Don't take anyone on the call unless they have an active role. And if you are taking multiple players, you might suggest that the prospect's appropriate counterparts be on hand as well. It is usually the case that the larger the group of players, the more the significance of the meeting. Plan well and use your resources wisely.

Set the appointment with your contact and discuss who else might need to be involved from your side or theirs. Discuss how much time you think you will need and agree on how much time is blocked so that you and he can plan accordingly. Also, clarify the purpose of the meeting, the concepts to be covered, and discuss any key items that may need advance planning. If it is a critical or complex meeting with multiple players, you may want to create an advance agenda with your prospect and provide it for all participants.

Now for the actual sales call. When I make sales calls and announce myself to the receptionist, I never sit down. The subliminal message is "I'm expecting to get in pretty quickly." On average it will decrease your wait time. And always be professional and courteous so that the gate-keeper might become an ally. Many times small talk and some relationship building with a receptionist can reap big rewards down the road.

When you get in the prospect's office or conference room, devote some time to rapport-building and warm-up. When we talk about behavioral styles in another chapter, we'll cover attention spans and how much time to devote to the process with different types of people. The next order of business might be to discuss any "carry-over items from your last appointment, then begin your needs analysis questions. Ask well-thought-out questions which challenge them to engage a serious depth of thought.

Use your best active-listening skills during your discovery process to maximize the quantity of useful information you are able to get from your prospect. Remember the better and more respectfully you listen and reflect on their responses, the better and more information you will get. Never begin your sales presentation without asking needs-analysis questions first. We have a chapter coming up on the best practices for performing the needs-analysis.

Too many salespeople start too low in an organization where the rejection is least likely to take place. That's fool's gold. I say start as close to the top as you can. The greatest referral you will ever get is one from the boss to his subordinate in the decision making loop! Have the courage to start high in the pecking order when you make a call, and, over time, you will be rewarded for that behavior. The "C Club" (as in CEO, CFO, COO) as it is often called is where the bigger thinkers and bigger budgets are found. Remember that the road is less traveled there, because most of your competitors start too low as well.

TUNE IN TO WIFM

You can bet that the customer or prospect is endlessly asking himself *What's in it for me? What will I get out of this relationship, this product, this presentation?* You need to let him know what's in it for him at the same time you must let him know that you care about his benefits and outcomes. Top salespeople concentrate on providing cutting-edge solutions, creating opportunities, and, in general, making customers feel good about the sale and the relationship. There have been some top professionals who actually refuse to take an order unless there is a definite match between their product or service and the customer's goals. Their focus on the customer goes well beyond lip service. This can be a powerful trust builder.

In contrast, average and below average salespeople never fully develop the skill. Instead, they seem more focused on their goals, even if those goals are reached at the expense of a customer. These people don't last in the profession of selling. As you monitor a customer's goals, keep in mind that many factors can serve as the "change agent." There may be changes in personnel, unexpected successes and failures within the organization, changes in their industry or market structure, involvement in a merger or acquisition, new technology, changes in their competitive environment or other factors. Insurance executive Ben Ward sends a charitable contribution to the favorite charity of his agents when they make their first sale through his company. It's an unexpected gesture but one that's never forgotten.

To build trust, you must create a low stress environment. You cannot pressure somebody one minute and expect them to trust you implicitly the next. Fifteen years ago, a lot of sales techniques created high stress and low trust. Today's sales professional is a master at keeping stress low and trust high.

High performers have character. You won't find many salespeople who endure for the long haul without it. What do we mean by "character"? This definition offered by Cavett Robert, the Chairman Emeritus of the National Speakers Association is a good one: "Character is the ability to carry out a resolution long after the mood in which it was made has left you." Strong resolve to do what you plan and say will set you apart from the masses. Strong producers seem to always be strong self-disciplinarians, and they keep promises.

A BRIGHT SPOT IN THE MIDDLE EAST

In 2011 my wife, Terri Murphy, and I were invited by the Society of International Business Fellows to be on the faculty of the Middle East Leadership Academy in Amman, Jordan. We were pleased to accept the invitation and spend two and one-half weeks at a luxury hotel on the Dead Sea with about 40 really sharp young Middle Easterners in an intense learning environment.

Most of them were western educated (Princeton, Harvard, etc.) and English-speaking, so that solved the language barrier issue. Their average age was probably 35. One of the best takeaways I got from the experience was observing the massive determination of these people to learn western leadership principles. They asked everyone on faculty if they could please share a meal with them so that they could ask more questions and gain a full understanding of what we were teaching.

Our MELA students displayed an uncanny ability to build trust in a short period of time, communicate with faculty members with great clarity and get from this course of study exactly what they came for.

The challenge for the faculty was to learn about the students and why they enrolled so that we could adapt to their needs quickly. We had to do some serious trust building in a short period of time as well, to make progress with them. We did it, established good goal-congruence, and had a fruitful win-win learning experience.

TIPS FOR COMMUNICATING IN A HIGH-TRUST RELATIONSHIP

To create exceptional relationships we need superb communication skills. Below is a list of things that help us prioritize in our effort to be an extraordinary communicator.

1. Lead with your ears! Be a great listener.

2. Control your emotions.

3. Carefully consider their agenda and assertions.

4. Take notes and give as much eye contact as practical.

5. On key issues, probe for additional information and understanding.

6. Summarize their comments at reasonable intervals for validation and clarity.

7. Try to discern their beliefs, intentions, and priorities.

8. Look for facts and feelings.

9. Tell your story in an easily understandable manner.

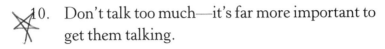

10. Don't talk too much—it's far more important to get them talking.

11. Make them feel important often, but don't be patronizing.

12. Encourage them as they speak by giving them positive non-verbal signals.

13. Be confident but not arrogant.

People sometimes withhold trust for self-protection. Don't give your customers a reason to protect themselves. Give them reasons to trust you.

If people must always be on guard with you or constantly be suspicious of your motives, selling to them will be a long and tedious process. In fact, you may never get a sale from an uncomfortable prospect. People will open up to you only when they truly trust you. We will only reveal our true feelings to the extent that we can anticipate understanding.

High performance salespeople develop a win-win strategy based on mutual trust. The essence of this strategy recognizes an important and fundamental truth: The best way for a sales professional to serve his own self-interest is to make sure that the customer's self-interest is served as well.

Success, the win-win strategist knows, depends on mutual satisfaction. We emphasize mutual satisfaction with a style that excludes manipulation. Another way is to allow yourself to lose so that the customer wins. Some salespeople do this all the time, usually in the vain hope that doing their customers such favors will pay off in the future. Accommodating your customers at your own expense is, in the long term, just as bad as not satisfying them at all.

A win-win approach to sales involves maintaining a delicate balance. It means keeping your customers happy without giving the store away. Total subservience and self-sacrifice do not have to be part of the formula.

So remember, authenticity is the order of the day. Authenticity pays off for both the customer and for you. How far are you willing to go in a relationship? How much energy are you willing to put in that relationship? Nothing worthwhile is easy to bring about.

> **Priceless**
>
> Dale Carnegie was right. To win friends and influence people we must talk in terms of the other person's interests. It was true when he wrote it, and even truer today for sales professionals trying to build trust and gain a competitive edge.

PART II

YOUR BLUEPRINT FOR SALES SUCCESS

CHAPTER FOUR

Goal Setting and Achievement

"Diligent planning leads to profit as surely as haste leads to loss."

SOLOMON

To further set the stage for our success in selling value, we need clarity of thought regarding our tasks at hand. If our simple goal is to *sell more*, that lack of focus will not serve us well. If your goal is to be the best value-based sales professional in your competitive region by year-end, for example, that will provide you with greater specificity in crafting your success plan, and developing the goals you will need to achieve, and the time frame in which to make it work. Assuming you have done your due diligence about what is transpiring competitively in your marketplace, you will be ready to move into your tactical approach to goal-setting.

BECOME PART OF THE UNCOMMON FEW

Setting goals is a powerful, life-changing process. As a sales professional it will make a tremendous difference in your production because you will have a framework in place that will simply require more of you on a daily basis. And it works! Would you be amazed to learn that less than one-half of 1% of the employed American work force has their goals in writing? Less than one out of two hundred! Perhaps we can get by without doing it, but don't get into that trick bag. Be among the uncommon few who vow to craft a better life by having goals and a plan to achieve them.

GOALS DEFINED

A goal is anything you want to do, be, have or achieve. All four of the elements in that definition imply that if you set goals you have a desire for progress in your life.

I love to ask sales professionals "What are you going to require of YOU this year?" Goal setting, when done right, is an inspiring and refined process of assuring personal accountability. When you have set your goals in writing you have begun the process of programming your subconscious mind so that it can work for you 24-7. Just by committing them to a document you have tripled your commitment to the goal and the probability of successful achievement. If you will also assign a time frame for achievement for each goal, you will quintuple your commitment and probability of success—great odds in anybody's book.

ZERO IN ON WHAT WORKS

The most committed and successful goal-setters write their goals down and assign a time frame to each. This is the habit I strongly suggest you develop. Here are some helpful tips for goal-setting success:

1. Make a document—write your goals down, either hard copy or in your computer, capture them in a form you can review often and stay committed to.

2. Thoughtfully craft your goals, by category, with detail, and with an eye on the big picture. It costs nothing extra to think big. Try to find that perfect mix of stretching within capabilities while staying in touch with reality.

3. Formulate and commit to new habits as required. Define what you must do differently and better going forward. I call them your "PHR"s—programmed habitual responses. These are habits you are willing to learn, internalize and commit to that are specifically designed to help you reach your goals.

4. Monitor results and recalibrate as necessary. Sometimes you will need to either fine-tune a goal or fine-tune your action plan to make

things work in harmony. These elements need to be synchronized.

5. The more detail the better! The more specifics you tie into your goals, the more vividly you will envision and focus on them.

6. Quantify your goals by types. This has to do with three time parameters: short-term—six months or less; intermediate—greater than six months, but less than two years; and long-term—two years or more.

7. Create a defined action plan. Put down exactly what you must do on a daily, weekly, monthly, and quarterly basis to make your plan become a reality.

THE POWER OF FOCUS

You have heard that you can take a newspaper outside in the hot summer sun, put a magnifying glass over it, and, as long as you slowly move it around, nothing will happen. But as soon as you hold it still, within a matter of seconds, it will begin to burn a hole in the newspaper. This is a great example of the power of focus. Humans behave similarly. When we are out of focus (no goals, no direction, no discipline) anything will distract us, as we bounce off the walls in all directions, influenced by many interrupting inputs, and get little or nothing done.

As soon as we get focused and have our goals in place, we are success machines in the making. We become less vulnerable to the daily ambiguities that come our way. What is the explanation of this phenomenon?

The best way I can explain this from my experience is as follows: first we accept that the human brain and its capabilities are miraculous, we perform best when both our conscious and subconscious minds are aligned and directed toward the priority tasks and goals we have in place. Our positive intent and solid focus take us into new realms; your brain then filters sensory input to keep you from being overwhelmed by the tens of thousands of inputs of varying descriptions that penetrate your brain on a daily basis. When, through your intentional focus, your goals are in place and your habits for achievement have become second nature, the reticular activating system in our brain serves as a "noticing apparatus" for you and the ideas, inputs and needed elements for progress start to miraculously come into play.

Professional speaker Jim Rohn spoke at our National Speakers Association Convention a few years ago. The best line of his talk, in my opinion, was "If something is important, work from document, not just thought." When we go to document we are telling our brain to notice what is important about this subject, and we begin to filter out useless peripheral information and concentrate on pertinent information. Write down the names of companies and people you want to attract into your life, and you will focus on the things that matter. It is miraculous how they will start to show up.

A FULL-TIME SERVANT AT NO CHARGE

Have you ever encountered people who say, "I don't need to write down my goals? They are right up here in my head, and that's good enough for me!" Some would argue that unwritten goals are better than no goals at all, but they would have overlooked the most important fact about goal setting: the human goal achievement process takes place in both the conscious mind and the subconscious mind. Unwritten goals are another success trick-bag. Don't fall for it because too much is at stake.

Once you have consciously gone through the process of developing your goals, you will have turned the achievement process over to your subconscious mind, as if putting it on automatic pilot. The subconscious mind, once programmed, works for you 24 hours a day, 365 days a year, and all it costs you is a little time and energy to program it. It's hard to believe we can have a full-time servant without cutting a check.

SET GOALS BY CATEGORY

Here is a recommended process that has proven to be a solid one if we follow it. It has to do with the eight goal categories for goal-setting. Some people have said "What does this material have to do with successfully selling value?" If we are working on a success plan to preserve our company's margin, and maximize our personal income by selling value with great effectiveness, I think we need to have balance in multiple aspects of our lives so that we can stay focused on the right things. If the rest of your life is not working, then neither are your career goals. The goal is life-balance. Here are the eight categories of goals for your consideration. I have listed them alphabetically:

- **Career goals.** The biggest enemy of the setting and achievement of career goals is complacency. Don't allow yourself to take opportunities for granted. Maintain a commitment to growth and advancement in this vital area. Get focused on the areas that matter most and develop a solid plan for progress.

- **Education and personal development goals.** We all need new skills and continued education to improve performance and quality of life. The mere fact that you are reading this book indicates you understand the importance of this category. Be eager and positive about developing your skills, and your life will continue to get better. The world is moving at incredible speed today. Don't let it outrun you!

- **Family goals.** To maintain a balanced, fulfilled life, you need to allocate energy in this area at all times. Again, the payoff can be great when the family unit works positively. The family is also customarily the most valuable source for a strong support system. Each family member can be an integral part of the success process for every other family member. I suggest you have periodic family meetings at which you discuss each other's goals and the progress being made toward them. Goals requiring the energies of all family members are especially valuable and important. By the way, I have never seen a high performing sales professional at his best while going through a divorce or dealing with major family problems. That can be the Godzilla of distractions. Develop the talent of reframing negative events and refocusing on positive possibilities.

- **Financial goals.** To neglect goal setting in this area is a serious miscalculation. In the area of financial goals, a little planning and discipline go a long way. They should focus on two key areas: net worth and income. Try not to contract what my friend Dr. Larry Markson calls the "I Need Disease." Financial progress is often based on the concept of our delaying gratification. Dave Ramsey even says don't buy anything if you don't have the cash, unless it's a home. Financial problems are another major source of distraction for those trying to advance their skill of value-based selling.

- **Physical goals.** You won't achieve the things you want to in life unless you are physically able to do so. Take care of yourself. Value and have pride in your body. Become a student of weight control, nutrition, exercise and your own metabolism. The healthier you are and the higher your energy level, the more you'll sell and the happier you will be.

- **Social, hobby and extra-curricular goals.** Once again, the word here is balance. Individuals vary greatly in their attitudes and needs in this category. Become aware of other family members' goals. Strive for compatibility. Ask yourself what hobbies and social involvements could be the most fun and rewarding. On the social side, the more people you meet and know the more substantial your personal network, which can be a great advantage to people in sales.

- **Spiritual goals.** Only you can ascertain your feelings, ideals and commitment in this category. I'll simply quote Dr. Kenneth McFarland who once said, "Few in any endeavor seem to endure over the long run without a meaningful spiritual conviction."

- **Community.** You make a living by working, but you make a life by giving. If you want a significant and successful life, give back to your community and the charities in it. It is impossible to out give yourself. If you are a giving person and don't even keep score (this is abundant thinking), happiness, and wealth will come around to play in your backyard just to give you more joy. Those who think they don't have the time or resources to give (this is scarcity thinking) are on the wrong track for a good life.

It is suggested that you spend nine days on your goal-setting process. Devote a day to each of the eight categories just discussed. Think about a given category for a full day, make notes, crystallize your thinking and focus on where you want your life to go in that area. The last day will be the time to put everything in final, organized form on your worksheet.

THE SPOKE-AND-WHEEL METHOD

In the next illustration you will see a wheel with eight spokes, one for each category of goals, and spokes numbered 1 through 10. Here is the process I recommend for successful goal-setting:

1. Consider your current reality. What grade do you give yourself in each of the eight categories? This will give you a snapshot of where you are starting from. Simply put a heavy dot on the hash mark next to the appropriate number. Let's say you put your dot for career goals on 7.

2. Now decide where you want to be at the end of this goal-setting period (whether one quarter, one year, five years, etc.). Now put an "X" on the number you want to be at the end of this period. We'll say you put and 8 down with an X. Do this in each of the eight categories. Note that the deviation between where you are and where you plan to be at the end of this period creates constructive tension and gives you the "fire in the belly" to proceed with energy and intent.

3. Now you are ready to start thinking and planning about what you want to set as specific goals in each of the eight categories.

4. List your goals on a separate page, marking them with the chosen time frame for its achievement.

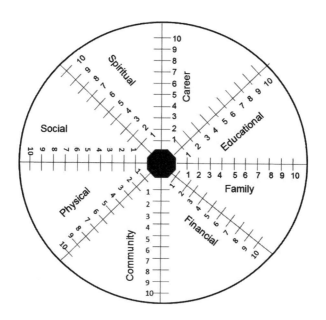

Theoretically, the best way to have a highly productive and balanced life is to be at a high number in each category so that when the wheel turns, you're covering a lot of ground and getting a smooth ride. If your eight categories were graded as 4, 9, 6, 1, 10, etc. and you drew a line from number to number in your illustration, you will have drawn a wheel that's going to give you a rough ride with limited achievement.

GOAL ACHIEVEMENT:
10 STEPS TO GET YOU FROM VISION TO REALITY

In his bestselling book *Release Your Brakes*, fellow Speakers Roundtable member Jim Newman says something that I like about setting goals for yourself. "Goals aren't simple conveniences. The human behavioral system requires goals for survival."

Even the most primitive man set goals, though he certainly didn't write them down. His first goal was to find enough food or water to make it through the day, or shelter to survive the winter storm. When his basic needs were met, he'd move on to higher goals, like finding someone to snuggle up to around the campfire.

Those goals that we haven't consciously set but move toward anyway are referred to as "absentia goals." They are natural and basic to our existence. If the only goals we have are absentia goals, then we behave precisely like Mr. Primitive. We move toward whatever has become the uppermost thought in our minds at any given time. We let the needs of the moment determine our agenda, instead of striving for well-considered, noble goals.

I've known people who behaved as though their goal was to fail. Clearly they didn't sit down and write "Goal One: Failure." But by failing to establish a goal structure for themselves, they began to move toward goals that were set by the first-thing-that-pops-into-my-mind method of setting goals. And that system is a first-class ticket to failure or, at best, to mediocrity.

Some people behave like they are going to live forever. They seem to never get around to doing the life-planning and goal-setting they need to do, thinking they've got plenty of time for that. Then they wake up one day to realize they are outliving their resources due to poor planning. Sad.

Now that your goals are presumably in place and you have engaged in the goal-setting process, you have things teed up for more accomplishment than ever. The visualization process you have engaged in has you ready for actualization now, so congratulations on getting this far. Now the plan is to enjoy higher achievement by ramping up not only your know-how but also your determination to follow through.

I hope the goals you have set have sufficiently inspired you to be ready to make some changes. As implied earlier, the habits we must internalize to improve our productivity will make all the difference. When our belief system is solidly in place, our behavioral process will begin to follow. Behavior is driven by those beliefs, and there is a need to craft or fine-tune new habits, which need to be so ingrained and internalized that we are using them on a daily basis.

Don't be afraid to set significant goals. Stretch yourself beyond previous levels—believe me, you have the capacity to do it—we can all improve when we decide to do so. There are no unrealistic goals, only unrealistic time frames.

By now, you know the importance of not only having a solid, well thought out plan, but also a willingness to make a commitment to the execution of that plan. Here are ten ideas to keep in mind for maximum achievement:

1. Organize the execution of your plan around the **numbers** you know you will need. In other words, consider your track record, and things like call count required to get appointments, and appointments required to get commitments, and so forth. There should be no question as to what you must do to make your goal become a reality.

2. Exercise the **discipline** needed to fully carry out your plan by meeting your numbers. If at any time you get behind on your plan, ramp up your call count to stay on track. Be accountable for your achievement process and persevere.

3. Leverage **relational capital** to make it happen. Consider those people who can help you move the ball forward, and get assistance from friends, clients, advocates, and colleagues in getting leads, appointments and assistance.

4. Monitor **time frames** of goals and results to be sure you are on track and adjust and re-calibrate as you need to.

5. Tap into your social **media connections** in any and every manner that can help you advance your cause and reach your goals. That can provide short cuts to high levels of achievement in many ways.

6. Reject the doubts and **negative influence** of others, and be determined in your efforts. There

will always be people who will cast doubt on your plan—that should be 'water off the duck's back'! Don't let it get to you.

7. Craft and adopt a **positive habit structure** which assures that you are performing at your highest proficiency level. Thrive on the constructive tension that has been created for you to achieve new levels of performance.

8. Make every call with an **inspired spirit** and an **attitude** that you will not be denied. And, if rejected, get over it fast!

9. Manage **your time** and efforts with a vengeance—start early, stay late, work hard, minimize breaks, and do the most important things in a timely manner.

10. Be respectful in **managing interpersonal relationships**, especially with customers. Always be a resource to others—never a burden, and you will be amazed how much they will help you!

THE POWER OF PRACTICING SELF-DISCIPLINE

High performers are competent self-disciplinarians. They have a stick-to-it dedication to the task at hand that paves the way for success after success. Keep in mind that discipline, intense desire and persistence determine our destiny, not simple wishes.

Sales managers building a team of winners want those salespeople who subscribe to the "I'll-Make-Just-One-More-Call" philosophy: Not the clock watchers who say, "Just one more hour and I can quit." Winners have the discipline to use every minute well. Energized professionals believe few people ever attain greatness by watching the clock!

It takes discipline to set the alarm at 5:30 a.m. instead of 6:00 a.m. It takes discipline to block out office distractions, to say no to the siren call of golf or long lunches or other enjoyable activities that can shorten the time you have available to spend working toward your goals.

It takes discipline to keep on keeping on, to keep pouring energy into that last 30 minutes of a long day. But high performance salespeople have that kind of personal discipline, and it makes the difference between mediocrity and greatness.

HABITS: COMMANDERS OF OUR DESTINY

Career success and goal achievement are seldom instantaneous. They normally occur over a significant period of time. When you map out the path you plan to take to reach your goals, you'll be taking the journey in small steps—minutes and hours and days and weeks that add up into years. And all during those minutes and hours and days, you'll be following your habits. They determine your probability for success. Is your habit structure one that will enable you to reach your aspirations?

Constantly assess and reassess your personal and professional habits. Recognize a bad habit for what it is: a roadblock on your success journey. Replace that roadblock with a well-thought-out productive habit that will propel you to your destination. Here's a three-step program that can help you in your efforts to replace undesirable habits.

> **Step One:** Write down the old habit you want to change. Suppose you've been sporadic about writing personal notes to prospects after an initial call. You know it's a valuable step that will make subsequent calls much more fruitful, so you vow to fix the problem.

> **Step Two:** Write down the new habit you're going to implement, and write the results you expect with this better habit. Get specific with a tactical approach like "I will write five hand-written notes to prospects or clients daily. I will do this early in the morning or at night and will not use valuable selling time for this activity."

> **Step Three:** Write the dates you'll start to work on this behavioral change, and the date you plan to have it totally internalized.

Habits are hard to change. That's why we recommend the written process. Writing it down helps you internalize your intentions and dramatically increase your chances of success. And, just as with written goals, writing down how you plan to change triples your commitment to sweep out habits that are holding you back and adopt new and better habits.

PERSISTENCE PAYS

I had the privilege of knowing and interviewing noted global entrepreneur and philanthropist, the late John B. Tigrett. He was incredibly successful, well-connected, and had some terrific stories to tell. As a world-class deal maker, he told me about one of his ventures that required a combination of extraordinary self-belief, patience, and persistence.

I had done a business deal for Armand Hammer in Morocco and had gotten to know him well. A couple of years later, when I decided to change my life and move to Europe, I asked him if he had any work I could do. So he got me to run his Occidental (Petroleum) operation in Europe.

One of the first things I saw was that he was very limited in the oil business. He had operations in California and in Libya, but Libya was very treacherous because of the political situation. So I suggested that he try to get into the North Sea.

Now the North Sea was not a very popular option at the time; it was regarded as too much of a gamble. They'd only found one well. But my own view about what was in the North Sea was this: an island of coal surrounded by a sea of oil.

Another deterrent to the North Sea was that getting the right to drill there was very political—and very expensive. You had to go to the government and sell them with great detail and conviction on why you *wanted this particular block of water to drill in. What we did was put two ships and a team of geologists out there and spent between $7 and $8 million finding out where we wanted to drill. We finally decided to try to get five blocks.*

Because getting the blocks was so political, I decided we needed somebody local on our team. We had Dr. (Armand) Hammer, and he had gotten Allied Chemical. I knew and had done work for J. Paul Getty, and I got him to come on board. While I was looking for somebody else, Lord Roy Thompson called me. He owned newspapers all over the world. I'd never met Lord Thompson, but of course I had heard of him. So he called me and said, 'Paul and Armand said that I need to talk to you. Come see me.'

I went to his place—it's like a castle—and I met this fellow, very thick glasses on, and he said, "Call me Roy." I asked why he had wanted to see me and he said, "I called you because I want to be worth a billion dollars before I die." Well, I can tell you that I'd never had anybody say that to me before! I said, "Roy, that's an unusual proposition. Let me ask you what you are worth right now." So Lord Thompson went over to his desk, pulled out this little drawer, looked at some papers and said, "This morning I was worth $616 million." I said, "That's great. We don't have so far to go!"

Then I told Lord Thompson that I only knew of two things in the world that you could make a billion dollars on: one was property, and the other was oil. That's when I thought, "By George, this is who I could get for the North Sea deal!" So I got Lord Thompson to join us.

We got this big drilling platform out of New Orleans and sent it over and we started to drill. We drilled that thing for about five weeks and it turned out to be the driest hole any of us had ever seen. And when you've got a dry hole 710 feet under water, you've got a really dry hole! And nothing you can do with it.

I had gotten Lord Thompson to put up $5 million and right away I got a call from him. "I heard the hole was dry," he said. "How much did that cost us?" I told him that it cost about $8 million. He started to talk about how I had assured him we'd find oil, but I reminded him that I'd always said it was a gamble.

From that dry hole, we went to the next one. Same partners, no change in our procedure, just moved the rig down to the next high and drilled about five weeks. That one was dry too: Moved on to the next high, drilled five weeks, another dry hole.

By this time we had had three dry holes, and I had just about lost Lord Thompson. He was calling me every day, getting real mean on the telephone too. Our losses were enormous at that point. But I just kept on telling him, "There's oil out there somewhere—and I want to keep drilling until we find it!"

I had this man working on the rig named Wilson. So we started on the fourth well and I said to Wilson, 'If

ness day with great expertise, before it starts. Include such elements as when you will make your first call and on whom, who else you will call on and in what sequence. Try to minimize "windshield time" and maximize "face time".

4. Include **Call Count** in your plan for that day. Decide in advance how many calls you intend to make and on whom. Don't let the emotion of the moment change your plan. Stick to it! Include what time you plan to make your last call. If you are on a roll try to add more calls into the mix; if running late, still try to do all you can to reach your call count for that day.

5. **Plan your week, month, and year** if you really want to excel, and don't let ANYTHING get in the way.

6. Give careful thought to your **Mode of Contact** in respect to each prospect. Is the next call on this person/company best handled by a personal call, social media, telephone call, or some other mode?

By the way, if you take a vacation, enjoy it and don't worry about or think too much about work. If you are working, don't be daydreaming about your vacation. It will only get you off track. Keep your head in the game and stay in the moment no matter what you are doing.

SHORT-CIRCUITING FAILURE, AND PLANNING FOR SUCCESS

In an earlier chapter I mentioned a study I spearheaded several years ago while on the Board of Sales and Marketing Executives International. We wanted to find out the "Failure Factors" of sales people, and we learned some fascinating things. The number-one failure factor of salespeople, we learned after performing an exhaustive survey was: *Salespeople have a tendency to improperly or inadequately organize their time and/or their sales efforts.*

Further research into this issue revealed that salespeople were not spending enough time in direct communications with their prospects and clients. We let things get us off track too often. Lack of planning equals lack of face, internet or phone time with prospects. I want to provide you with a time management tool now which will help you in that regard. We have divided the time management function up into four categories.

The first is **"A-Time."** A-Time is time spent in direct communications, in person, on the phone, or online with prospects or customers. Nothing is more important than A-Time and an insufficient quantity of it will take us down quicker than anything else. So, make the calls, talk to the people, and things will happen!

The second category is **"B-Time."** B-Time is time spent in preparation for more productive A-Time. For example, as you participate in this course of study, your desired outcome is to learn skills for the improvement of your sales results. So it's doing the things that will help you make your all-important A-Time more successful.

The third category is **"C-Time."** C-Time is for all other business activities. This will entail such things as drive time from call one to call two, paperwork, essentially anything else you need to do that does not include A-Time or B-Time activities.

The fourth category is **"D-Time."** D-Time is personal time. I have known salespeople who have devoted so much time to A, B and C items that they ended up neglecting their family. Work to keep a good life balance. You may want to re-visit the chapter on goal setting to perfect this one.

IMAGINATION AND CREATIVITY: GO FOR THE BIG ONES

Legendary billionaire, J. Paul Getty was being inter-viewed on his deathbed when a London reporter asked Mr. Getty if he would have done anything differently in his life. Getty replied "I have had a good life. I would not change much but, if anything, I think I would have gone for bigger deals." He was reported to be the wealthiest man in the world at that time. I give him really high marks for thinking big.

If you want to become a high-performance salesperson who makes the really big sales, you'll have to throw away your blinders and put on a wide-angle lens. You'll need to be willing to try new, fresh, unusual, and unique approaches to each sales opportunity. You'll need to use imagination. And most importantly, you need to become the kind of thinker who can confidently prepare, make the big call, and make a positive impression in the process.

There are millions of conscientious people who put in long hours and do their jobs with diligence but never reach significant levels of achievement. One thing that may hold these people back is they don't imagine as hard as they work. They just keep repeating yesterday one more time. Salespeople who get the big ticket sales usually do so with innovative approaches. They're the people who are engaged in an endless quest for more creative ways to get people to say "Yes!"

Anyone who is not periodically experiencing a failure or setback is probably not trying anything to test his or her potential or to stretch their vision and track record of achievement.

THE CREATIVITY WITHIN YOU

Many subscribe to the belief that we come into this world with naturally flowing creativity. How sad it is that many young people quickly get their minds cluttered with demands, barriers and creativity-squelching instructions, often from mediocre minds who wield power over kids' imagination and spontaneity because of their power, position or adulthood.

The corporate marketing department which, in its finest hour, creates a "Category of one" by uniquely and innovatively going to market with something exciting and new is to be admired. Salespeople need to stretch into similar thinking. If the educators who say we only function on

16-18% of our brain power are correct, perhaps it is time for us to kick on the after-burners and ramp up our expectations through our own efforts.

Bill Gove, my friend and mentor, said success for many people can mean uncluttering, tossing out limiting thoughts, previously-established barriers, and any other behaviors that tend to get in our way.

Next time you're looking for a new way to make a sale, increase your prospect list, or solve a problem for a client, free yourself from mental locks. If an idea comes to you, don't drop it just because it's not logical, not practical, or you just haven't done it before. Creativity begins when you stop saying "It can't be done" and start saying "Why not?"

Have you ever heard someone say, "Boy, he has quite an imagination!" That's often said in a critical way. But imagination is a positive trait, not a negative one. Imagination gives birth to creativity.

TEAR IT DOWN?!

My close friend, Ira Hayes, once told me a story about a man who never let comments like "That's not practical" or "That doesn't follow the rules" hold him back. He was great salesman and leader John H. Patterson, founder of NCR Corporation. Patterson, recognized by many as the father of professional selling, was a genius at creating visual aids and high impact examples to convey a sales point or message.

Sometime around the turn of the twentieth century, Patterson invited his top salesmen to Dayton, Ohio for a meeting. One night they had a beautiful dinner party in one of the buildings that made up the NCR complex.

After dinner, Patterson said to his men, "This has been a fine evening, and now the carriages are waiting out front to take you downtown to your hotel. I look forward to seeing all of you back here in this dining room tomorrow morning for breakfast." They said goodnight and departed.

What they didn't know was that Patterson had dozens of men standing by with horses, tools, shovels, sod and flowers. As the men drove away, Patterson had his work crew tear down the building, haul everything away, level the ground, lay the sod and plant flowers where the building had been. The next morning the salesmen came in the carriages for breakfast. Patterson was standing nearby, watching their faces as they arrived. They were astonished. Dumbfounded! Where was the building?

Then John Patterson stepped forward and said to them, "I wanted some way to help you remember that you should get things done quickly and be dramatic in your presentations. I thought this might be a way to make my message memorable." Boy, was it ever!

IMAGINATION IMPRESSES PROSPECTS

One way to make the biggest sale of your lifetime is to identify your prospect's biggest problem and come up with a creative solution to that problem. Find an answer that no one else has presented to him. It's likely that you will view the problem from an entirely different perspective than your prospect and therefore you may be able to show him solutions he hadn't considered.

Someone once asked Mark Twain, "How do you come up with those wonderful ideas and thoughts I've seen in your writings?" Mark Twain replied, "The process is simple. You sit down with pen and paper and write them down as they occur to you. Writing them down is easy—it's the occurring that's so hard."

To think and plan how you will creatively make a big sale requires expending positive energy, limiting distractions, and focusing on the customer and his situation in a special way not previously considered. Depth of thought, without barriers or preconceptions, will help you achieve a positive intensity in this process.

Of course you will never consistently make the big sales without skill and knowledge. But Einstein once said, "Imagination is more important than knowledge; for centuries, thousands of good ideas have received tremendous criticism from mediocre minds." Einstein makes a good case for imagination outweighing knowledge, but I also believe we cannot perform beyond our knowledge base. Knowledge is the soil and imagination is the seed, action is the water, so pour it on!

CONFIDENTLY PROCEED

The Wall Street Journal, in their Saturday Soapbox section recently interviewed tennis great Andy Murray and others about the importance of confidence. Murray said:

"The ones with the most success tend to have the most confidence. But success isn't the only measure of confidence – a lot of it has to do with authenticity and how you feel about yourself. When I was younger, I used to play against a lot of kids who were older and bigger than I was, especially my brother, Jamie, who always used to beat me. I think that instilled determination in me to win. It's often hard to explain a loss and often even harder to take it, but it happens to everyone, and as long as you learn from it, the defeats can sometimes be beneficial. After I lost my first Grand Slam, I struggled with confidence. I was quite young and desperate to win a Grand Slam, and I fell short. But it didn't affect my hunger to win, and despite losing a few more finals after that, I finally won. Perseverance and determination are key."

That quote tells us to remember that you never lose until you give up. Yes, self-management and perseverance are huge keys to success.

EMBRACE THE NO-LIMIT ASSUMPTION

A common characteristic of high-performance salespeople is that they don't limit their vision. They have learned to extend themselves into the no-limit realm.

These people don't short-circuit their potential power with poor expectations and limiting beliefs. They decide what they wish to achieve, and then they find a way to achieve it. Don't tell these people it's never been done or can't be done. For the high performer, "never been done" is a challenge, not a deterrent.

One way to keep from negating the success you hope to enjoy in the future is to expect a lot of yourself. Success comes when we have high expectations followed by a realistic game plan or strategy for making our vision real. Most people who are sitting around just waiting for their ship to come in never sent a ship out!

Extend yourself to your limits. And since you don't know what your limits are, just assume you don't have any. One of the principal ingredients in making the big sale is your expectation that you can. Remember the words of hockey great, Wayne Gretzky..." Every shot you don't take is a potential goal that you will never make!" None of us tend to exceed our expectations. If we do, it's usually accidental or some unanticipated catalytic agent enters the picture.

The high-performance salesperson proactively and continuously works on his self-image and expectations. He takes charge; mediocre salespeople tend to be reactive. They wait for things to happen and then respond in a very predictable manner.

STIFLE THE STIFLERS!

To think about possibilities instead of just problems, and get your imagination and creativity flowing, you need to understand that the impetus of innovation is optimism. Don't get short-circuited or stifled on your way to high achievement. Here's a list of the creativity stiflers to overcome:

1. Negative self-talk. Rid your vocabulary of phrases like "I've never done it that way" or "I couldn't do that" or "Nobody could accomplish that." This kind of talk is useless and damaging to your personal potential. Learn to replace those negatives with "I'm going to do it somehow, and I will find the how!" and similar positive responses.

2. Complacency. When a salesperson gets wrapped up in routine, repetitive activities and procedures that offer little or no payoff, it's nearly impossible to be creative and develop innovative strategies for setting new records.

Do you go to the coffee shop at the same time every day, sit with the same people and talk about the same things? Do you always do your tasks in the same order? And exactly the same way? Did you establish for yourself some pattern that worked last year or two or three years ago, and so you figure "If it ain't broke, don't fix it?" If so, you've become complacent. Sometimes it's better to break things and start over!

Make a vow now that each year you will seek a new and better way to perform the tasks you did last year. Or maybe find better tasks to be working on! Just making yourself look at old routines and seek new approaches is likely to provide you with new ideas for success. Examine every aspect of your professional life and expand your horizons.

3. Fear of failure/giving up. Each morning, look at yourself in the mirror and repeat these words: "The only people who never fail are the ones who never try anything." Remember that you can never fail if you never give up. When you miss that big sale, say to yourself, "I didn't get it today, but I've got tomorrow to try again." And say that again and again and again, until you succeed. High performers persevere.

4. Worrying what others might think. So often people go through life devoting endless hours wondering "What will they say if I...?" And then finally one day the person who was holding himself back realizes that "they" didn't really think much about him at all. Oh, they may have had some knee-jerk criticism or comment, but soon they forgot. Is it worth stifling your potential to win the approval of "they" (whoever they are)?

HIGH-IMPACT IMAGINATION

When I was involved with the Positive Thinking Rallies tour, I was afforded the wonderful opportunity of getting to know the legendary W. Clement Stone. I always enjoyed studying this billionaire and his uniqueness.

One day I found myself sharing a limousine with him from our hotel to the arena in San Diego. Stone was in his

70s, but he had lost none of his impressive powers. I was decades younger and not comfortable addressing him as "Clem," as some of his contemporaries did. So I said, "Mr. Stone, do you plan to retire soon or do you still have some compelling goals to achieve?"

Stone looked at me with those dark, piercing eyes. He slowly and deliberately took his Cuban cigar out of his mouth and said, "I still have one goal that I plan to achieve. It's simple. I want to change the world and make it a better place in which to live."

I was surprised, impressed, and temporarily silenced. I remember that conversation as though it were yesterday. It had a profound effect on me and made me realize the value and importance of having a personal mission and thinking big. It also reminded me that age is little more than a state of mind.

To complacently spend our days without a purpose that inspires or challenges us is to go through life without really living. Expect great things of yourself and tap into your creative energy!

SEE IT BIG!

We've discussed several ideas designed to enable you to focus on a bigger picture and gain greater results than you dreamed possible. Now I want to help you begin thinking with increased imagination and creativity about what you can do in the future. Here are some suggestions:

Begin to work harder on yourself than ever before. By that, I mean work diligently to expand your self-image and expectations. Your sales skills, your personal goals and objectives, your personal image and level of professionalism—all of these are vital. Remember this: Until you work hard on yourself any other hard work will not bring you as great a return.

Dramatically increase your focus toward your prospects, their needs, their desires, and what they value. You were probably doing a good job of this before you began reading this book. But now you need to give yourself a significant competitive edge by doing it even more. Focus on your prospects better and more consistently than your competition. See the big picture and work to find creative solutions to your prospects' big problems.

Never again be reactionary and narrow in your understanding of human behavior. Respect the dignity and individuality of everyone you call on, and be dedicated to the process of developing individualized, targeted strategies. You will be handsomely rewarded for the creativity you devote to this effort.

Put yourself a cut above the rest of the marketplace with an extraordinary level of service. Vow to maximize contacts and perfect your system of following up and following through. Give them attention and personal service beyond anything they have ever expected.

COMMUNICATING FOR SALES EFFECTIVENESS

Wars have been waged, marriages destroyed, enterprises lost, and relationships of all types strained to the limits due to poor communications. If you develop cutting edge communications skills, you have a good chance of advancing relationships with your prospects and customers. Dedicate yourself at every opportunity to learn, internalize and successfully use the best skills you can to be a superb communicator! We need every bit of skill we can muster to outperform our competition as we go into the marketplace to sell our unique value proposition.

We will look at several aspects of communications in this chapter that will help you minimize or eliminate the everyday problems salespeople experience in the flow of communications. First let's consider four critical aspects of communications:

1. Quality—Rule number one in communications is to be certain that it takes place! What is transmitted is what needs to be received. And we need to verify that it is a problem-free, well-understood interchange. The more important the subject, the more important the verification!

2. Timeliness—I wonder how many sales have been lost by salespeople failing to follow up in a timely manner thus losing opportunities. Be an absolute bear about scheduling your communications to keep promises and be on time.

3. Frequency—Try to make good decisions on how often you need to be in touch with prospects and clients. You want to be in touch when needed, staying ahead of the power curve, not getting usurped by competition, and exceeding

prospects' expectations with the accuracy and timing of your contacts.

4. Medium—Make every attempt to communicate with prospects and customers the way they want to be communicated with. It is incumbent upon YOU to find out the medium preferred. You need to ask each of them "What method of communication do you prefer?" You will often be surprised when they answer. Sometimes you will have a sixty-five year old say "Just text me", and a twenty-five year old say "Just give me a call on my cell." Others might prefer snail mail on some issues, and many will want to communicate through their preferred online medium. Even the old fax is still requested on some fronts. Go with their preference.

The words we use and how we say what we say are important, but facial expression and non-verbal behavior have the highest impact on others. A few years ago, Dr. Albert Mehrabian pioneered the concept of comparative analysis of verbal and non-verbal communications and verified that 55% of a message pertaining to attitude and feelings is in facial expression and non-verbals. Only 7% is about the words we choose, and 38% is how we say what we say. Think about this as you consider the basic, yet profoundly important advice of smiling and being pleasant in your demeanor when you talk to people.

We are also in an era whereby communication channels are not limited to in person and telephone sales calls, but by multiple additional channels - all requiring the skills of engagement, connection and ultimately conversion. These skills are really important, so you don't want to get behind the power curve on this one! Both online and traditional communication tools have the same objectives, and that is clarity and positive outcomes.

Don't assume all recipients will open and read all emails, don't use email alone—some people don't check their email regularly, and may be among those who prefer texts or social media. And use systems to verify that your important communique was received.

With multiple channels to choose from, don't assume that everybody participates in every element of social media. Monitor and research to determine what modes your better clients prefer. Communication requires response, and in today's world, often immediate response. Be very proactive about responding on the online channels you and your clients may be using, because no response will most likely result in no sale.

Now let's talk about the use of the telephone in our communications flow. It will continue to be a major medium for a long time, so let's vow to use it with maximum effectiveness. Here are fifteen tips for effective telephone communications for you to use for best results:

1. Always be sure to be the last one to hang up. How many times have you, near the end of a call, said the person's name to ask them one more question, but the salesperson has already hung up? Pause to be sure they've hung up first.

2. Speak clearly with the mouthpiece near your mouth.

3. Never interrupt. Remember, when two people are talking at once, communications is not taking place! So don't talk when the other person is talking, even if he interrupted you! The goal is clear understanding.

4. Always give thought to the BEST TIME to call. You may want to ask them when they want you to call. By the way, one clever tip I learned years ago was to try to call either before the bosses secretary arrived, or after they left—many times that boss will pick up his or her line.

5. Consider rate of speech. Mirror them as best you can, based on whether you are having a discussion with a fast-talker or a slow-talker.

6. If making an outgoing phone call and asking for Mr. Gary Bradshaw (for example), don't ever follow his greeting with your name and then "How are you today?" That's deadly. One hundred percent of the time they know you are calling to try to sell them something. Never, never, never say those words. Even saying something similar is much better, like "I hope you are having a good day." I'm personally more in favor of identifying yourself, your company, and then the purpose of your call with (hopefully) some kind of benefit statement in there somewhere.

7. Have an engaging, unique opening. Don't say what everybody else does.

8. Many telephone selling experts think it is better to ask them "Did I catch you at a bad time?" …than "Is this a good time?" Try both and see what works best for you—just don't say "How are you today?"

9. Clarify, in your mind, the purpose and objective of your call before making it. It's like goal-setting—the more clarity you have, the better the chance you will be successful.

10. Understand Telesales Momentum—If you're on a roll, keep on! Don't break the positive momentum, because it is a precious commodity. On the other hand if you are suffering from negative momentum and it's not going well, I recommend three things. First, reassess your techniques and the words and phrases you are using, and alter them as needed for more comfort and impact. Second, increase your activity by making more calls; third, turn on your optimism afterburner! Expect more results and they tend to follow; the worst thing you can do is to go into "Poor me mode" —there is no room in the success formula for self-pity!

11. Use the internet to facilitate your telephone sales activity. Visit prospects' website and online presence before calling. You will usually learn something that will be helpful to you during the conversation and advance the sales process.

12. Study your "File-to-date" info to recall the interchange you had with this person on the last call and be sure to build on previously gathered information. Doing your homework in pre-call planning always helps.

13. Be an intense note-taker during phone calls. Capture all of the pertinent data you can that will help you on ensuing calls. Personal data capture is also good—spouses and/or kids' names, reference to preferences in sports teams can be helpful. Perhaps a headset with notes taken on your computer could work best for you.

14. Watch your grammar and vocabulary. Grammatical errors are five times as deadly on the phone as they are in person. Try to match the vocabulary you use to the intellect and educational level of the person you are calling.

15. Stand up. Physiologists say that we think 2-5% faster standing up than we do sitting down. Anytime I am making a really important call or during a teleseminar, I always stand! You will engender higher energy, think quicker, and improve your response.

THE MARKET-SHARE MODEL

In this era of intense competition among sales organizations, much of our planned revenue gains must come from gaining market share from our competitors. It is a reality that we are constantly compared to our competition and how we are perceived in our arena with multiple peers. We need to understand the competitive dynamic of market share. If we know and use the associated control points we can seize opportunities and gain the share we want.

As competition continues to get keener we must get better than we've ever been. As we previously discussed, the bar of excellence is going up on all of us and we cannot expect acceptable levels of success from yesterday's skills. Exceptional selling skills and the crafting of new, customer friendly, cutting-edge solutions is the way of the future.

The top salespeople understand that the purpose of a business is to attract and retain customers. So we need to work on both increasing sales AND retaining existing customers.

Let's now discuss U. S. Learning's "Market-Share Model" and how we can develop an approach to gain market share. This model has basic but very important implications. It looks simple with the circle representing your market and the slice of the pie representing your market share.

It has some moving parts we need to address. There are four of them which can have an effect on your market share. Some are controllables and some are uncontrollables.

First, there is Market Expansion, which is an uncontrollable. The market is based more on economic conditions and external forces than anything we can do anything about it. We just know it's good news when it happens and we need to try to get our share of the economy's gains.

Secondly, there is Market Contraction, which is also an uncontrollable. It would nice if we could personally direct the economy and thus prevent the market from declining, but we can't. It's not good news, but we must periodically deal with it.

Third, we have the Front Door to your market share, which is a controllable. To increase market share we must bring more business through the front door. This could come from more business from existing customers, or new business from new customers.

Fourth, is the Back Door to your market share, which is also largely a controllable. You must do everything you can to keep customers from going out that back door. Customer turnover can be very costly, so having a proactive plan to keep customers happy is just as important as getting a new one!

The Market Share Model

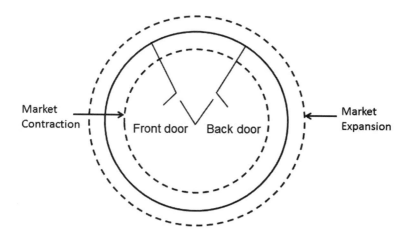

If we can maximize our front-door business development activities, and simultaneously slam our back door, eliminating or minimizing our customer turnover, we can increase the size of the angle representing our market share!

So let's heed the advice of psychologists who tell us not to endure a lot of brain damage over things we cannot control. It is a waste of valuable energy. Let's do what we know can work—provide great sales solutions and service to outperform our competition!

This entire program is about what we can do to bring more business through that front door. On the issue of slamming the back door, be aware that it is six times more expensive to get a new customer as it is to keep an existing one. So how do we behave to keep them happy?

Here are four tips to do it:

1. Stay keenly aware of their definition of VALUE, and what they say their needs and desires are. With that knowledge, craft strategies that will work for those customers.

2. Perform periodic customer service miracles for them that make them say "Wow"!

3. Gather intel that keeps you informed as to what your competitors are doing. By the way, what is the best source of that information? It's your really loyal customers who will share that information with you. Don't ever take for granted that your competitors are out there every day,

trying just as hard as you in many cases, to get YOUR market share!

4. Be an absolute BEAR about communications with your prospects and customers! Use every skill in this course of study as well as what you have learned in your years of experience to stay in touch with customers and anticipate their needs at all times. That, in and of itself, can be a powerful differentiator.

> **Priceless**
>
> Stretch yourself! Make that big call you've hardly thought about until now. Use a bold, imaginative approach. Expect success, work hard and smart, and make the sale. Celebrate your success, then initiate plans for an even bigger sale.

CHAPTER SIX

How to Build a Loyal Following

"Every customer touch point is a moment of truth for your company. Make it a positive experience every time and you will earn their loyalty."

JAN CARLZON

Occasionally you hear clients say something like this: "What I really like about John and his colleagues at Orbit Circuits is that they know exactly what I want, need and value, so we don't have to play games in our relationship." When you devote the time to find out all you need to know to make high quality recommendations, the payoff can be huge. This behavior is the pathway to earning the loyalty of your clients.

GAINING CUSTOMER LOYALTY

We all need to have a high level of awareness of the potential and current status of everybody in our database. Your database represents your "Book of Business", and you need to manage it as one of your most treasured assets. The "Loyalty Ladder" will give you a framework for categorizing everyone you are doing business with or would like to. As you master your use of the Loyalty Ladder, you will also become keenly aware of the current status of each entry, as well as the logical next steps to advance your relationship.

Some say loyalty is out of style. Companies are losing half of their customers in five years, half their investors in one year, and half their employees in four years! This lack of loyalty can be an absolute threat to growth and prosperity. Your job as a sales professional is to do everything you can to serve your company and your clients as best you can with your eye on the future. The greatest way to gaining loyalty is to create value for customers. I mean value by THEIR definition.

If you retain their loyalty and their business you can think of your income as "Royalties from Loyalties." The more loyal customers you have the less advertising and new prospecting you have to do. Imagine if you were so busy handling existing customers and their referrals that you had absolutely no time to make new calls. That would be a prosperous, high performance sales career.

THE LOYALTY LADDER

In this chapter, there are six categories of people on what is called the "Loyalty Ladder." I was introduced to this idea by my friend Murray Raphel who, along with Ray Considine, developed and researched the concept years ago. I have updated it somewhat and added another rung to the ladder.

Rung 1: The Suspect

The individual at the bottom of the Loyalty Ladder is the one we call the suspect. A suspect is an individual or organization who may or may not know about you or your company and may or may not be qualified to buy.

There are usually lots of suspects, and you'll have to work hard to find out which suspects can be moved into the second category on the scale. Normally the only way you can find out is to make calls and talk to people.

Rung 2: The Prospect

The second rung on the ladder is the prospect. A qualified prospect often knows of you or at least your company and, in your opinion, has the ability to buy. This person should be cultivated.

As you work on these prospects, you'll face the true challenge of selling. This is the crucial point when you are critically compared with your competition and evaluated. You'd better be at your best if you're going to move prospects into the third category.

Rung 3: The Customer

A customer is someone who has bought from you or your company at least once. That's a simple enough definition, but many salespeople never grasp the fact that often the easiest sale is one to an existing customer. It can frequently be your best source of additional business.

You probably have lots of customers to whom you could or should be selling more than you are, either in terms of volume or items in your line. Think about it and I'll bet you'll find some immediate business within your existing customer base. Customers become better profit centers when they become clients.

Rung 4: The Client

The fourth category is the one into which we want to move the customer, the category of client.

A client is someone who trusts and respects your judgment and accepts your advice. Professional salespeople have clients who consider them a valuable resource. Average salespeople develop very few. They seldom get beyond the customer category.

The high-performance salesperson is a master at developing maximum levels of business from his or her prospect and customer base. Clients should never be taken for granted, and you should try to turn those clients into advocates, our fifth category.

Rung 5: The Advocate

An advocate is someone who believes so strongly in you and your products and services that they eagerly buy from you everything that fits their needs and even send you unsolicited referred leads. An ability to develop relationships to the advocate level is the reason high-performance salespeople make strong sales performance look easy. In a very selective way, you may try to move advocates into your final category on the ladder.

Rung 6: The Confidant

The confidant stands at the top rung of the Loyalty Ladder. This is someone with whom you have a special and very close relationship. The confidant freely and unselfishly gives and takes private advice, with your best interests and friendship being a prime consideration. This relationship requires a great deal of time and commitment to develop and maintain.

Some people may go a lifetime and never have a confidant. Some may have several. A confidant buys from you with an unspoken, natural, flowing commitment that often includes all of their business. This relationship is the ultimate in terms of in-depth, loyal, authentic communication. If you are fortunate enough to have any such relationships you should treasure them.

MANUFACTURING GOOD LUCK

Perhaps you have seen a salesperson who succeeded magnificently and everyone says, "Oh sure, she's got the such-and-such account. She's had it for years. I'd be making big bucks too if I had that account. She is simply lucky."

Well, critics usually have no idea of the energy, effort and unselfish commitment that goes into such a relationship. In that situation, the successful salesperson is usually selling either to an advocate or confidant. As you work on relationships in your territory or marketing area, try to continually upgrade each person's status relative to the six categories we have just discussed. It's an opportunity to manufacture your own good luck.

To move people up the Loyalty Ladder, it is recommended you follow a specific procedure. First, perform an analysis and profile of your current business base by putting each account in one of the categories just defined. Next, mark the twenty percent best prospects in terms of potential. Finally, work to move each targeted account up to the next rung on the ladder.

If you're not making progress work diligently on relationship skills and focus more intently on customer goals and needs. The higher you move a customer up the Loyalty Ladder, the shorter your selling cycle will become and the less competition will be an issue. Speaker and trainer Don Thoren says, "All relationships and their accompanying psychological contracts are being continuously renegotiated, whether we acknowledge it or not." Always maintain respect for those you deal with, and continually ask yourself, "How can I be more valuable to them?"

KEEP ADDING TO THE PIPELINE

To keep your pipeline viable you must be adding new accounts to the pipeline on a consistent basis.

Adding new accounts will normally require an organized process of making cold calls. Keep in mind that making cold calls can contribute significantly to your growth process and ultimate level of success. You really don't have anything to lose by making the call, and you might realize substantial gain. If you don't consistently make some new calls, you just may wake up one day and find yourself with no one to talk to.

Many salespeople are reluctant to make that first cold call. There are two simple reasons for this. One is that the salesperson feels rather negative about calling on suspects or marginal prospects because of the time that it normally takes to get an order from them. That type of call has the longest selling cycle. The second reason is that salespeople know that the farther down the scale a prospect is located, the greater the probability of rejection. As discussed earlier, many salespeople handle rejection poorly and don't want to risk it. There's one sure way to avoid it. Quit making calls, but be prepared to face the consequences.

SET YOURSELF APART FROM YOUR COMPETITION

Sometimes the non-traditional approach to something will draw new interest levels and a unique following. Before you laugh at what appears to be an off-the-wall approach to achieving your goal, look behind you to see if anyone is following you to hear what you have to say.

Have you developed a creative approach to capturing the intrigue of others, or are you among those in need of a charisma transplant? Set yourself apart with a noble cause that others will admire. It can be as captivating as the establishment of a new charitable institution or as basic as a sales idea or customer service technique that is admired by all.

Stanley Mills, one of the most successful real estate sales professionals I know, once heard that a primary reason for the erosion of a client base is that salespeople do not adequately stay in touch with their clients and prospects. Stanley not only sends his clients birthday and Christmas cards, but he also calls each man in his data base, three days before his anniversary, to remind him of the upcoming event. You won't be surprised to learn that it's the only such call they get that day.

WHERE DID ALL MY COMPETITORS GO?

Almost every business and industry operating today is becoming more competitive. But, on a personal level, I'm convinced we can consistently beat our competition. How? By being so relationship-focused and personally proficient at moving our customers to the higher levels of the Loyalty Ladder that the majority of our business is on the top three rungs.

On the bottom three rungs, you are dealing with people who will cut your throat for a hundred dollar bill! (Well, almost.) The competition is fierce down there, and you are just one more member of the masses. Get your customers to the higher rungs on the ladder, and you will be one of the elite big hitters who devote your time and energies to substantive client issues and problems. Remember, the higher you climb on the ladder, the less vulnerable you are to the competition!

Do everything you have learned to stay in touch with people in your database and move them up the Loyalty Ladder; remember: "out sight—out of mind."

Make strategic decisions regarding the frequency of calls on the people in your database. Remember, while you are deciding whether to call on them or not your competitor probably is. Even if someone on your list is currently giving most of their business to a competitor, you want to be next in line when the current vendor screws up. So stay in touch at appropriate intervals and nurture the companies along that you think could represent excellent opportunity down the road.

Priceless

Patiently nurture customer relationships with greater creativity and sensitivity than your competitors, and they will be calling each other trying to figure out what you are doing that is destroying their market share!

PART III

UNDERSTANDING YOUR CUSTOMER

CHAPTER SEVEN

The Psychology of Selling

"Everybody's weird once you get to know 'em."

"BROTHER" DAVE GARDNER

THE GENESIS OF BEHAVIORAL STYLE THEORY

After reading many books, being a student of human behavior for some forty years and consulting with multiple behavioral scientists, I feel comfortable that I have arrived at solid conclusions regarding behavioral styles and their application to selling.

Many agree that human behavior is what you see and hear people say and do. That presents a relatively simple thesis we can readily use: We can observe the behavior of a person and gain predictability about them that is useful in a selling situation.

Believe it or not, Hippocrates identified four behavioral styles in approximately 400 B. C., which, amazingly, are comparable to the most popular style grids today. We're going to approach the behavioral side of selling in a manner that will enable us to take advantage of the many years of research that have been done.

In more recent history, Dr. Carl Jung formulated much of the early research in the behavioral sciences. Renowned psychologist Dr. David Merrill and many others have had an impact on the development of the behavioral style models that have proven to be valuable to sales professionals today.

Larry Wilson, Tony Alessandra, Don Thoren and I (though not psychologists) have burned the midnight oil as well, studying human behavior.

HARD SCIENCE VS. SOFT SCIENCE

It is important to point out the human behavioral sciences are a "soft science", which means that while predictable, they are not exacting and are imperfect. A hard science is exacting. To illustrate the difference between a hard science and a soft science, if I drop a pencil from a standing position, we all know it will hit the floor. The law of gravity is exacting and irrefutable. It works every time.

It's more difficult to make irrefutable statements about human behavior, but we have learned a great deal about it. And now behavioral scientists can, in most instances, predict how certain types of individuals will behave in certain situations. When a sales professional has this knowledge it can be enormously valuable.

HUMAN BEHAVIORAL RESEARCH

We're going to approach the behavioral side of selling in a manner that will enable us to take advantage of the many years of research that have been done. Behavioral scientists including B. F. Skinner practiced the process by watching people and describing what they *do*. He did not make an attempt to analyze *why* a person behaved in a certain manner.

This is different from Dr. Sigmund Freud, a psychoanalytical theorist who sought to understand what a person *is*, and the motivation for his behavior. Freud, with his works related to the id, ego, and superego, was the founder of this school of psychology.

We are going with the Skinner model in this book and will focus on observing the behavior of others to gain predictability so that we might increase the probability of successfully dealing with them.

SELL DIFFERENT PEOPLE DIFFERENTLY

If you want to be a high-performance salesperson, you simply cannot fall into the trap of trying to sell all prospects the same way. Wouldn't it be great if all prospects behaved in exactly the same manner? If they did, sales training and the development of persuasive skills would be relatively easy.

We have recognized that it isn't that simple. Have you ever made a call on a prospect with whom you felt immediate rapport and comfort, and it resulted in you making a sale on the first call on them? Have you ever called on someone with whom you felt no immediate rapport, and had difficulty communicating with them? Perhaps there was no variability in your approach, but your results were totally different. You departed the first scenario on cloud nine thinking you were one great sales professional. You left the second call thinking that prospect was "weird!" Let's discuss this incident in greater depth.

What's a good, one word definition of "weird"? Odd, strange, different—all of these are good. Here's the premise: *The more ways people are different from each other, the more effort will be required to communicate and to achieve a mutually acceptable outcome from the interpersonal relationship.* That's a rather formal behavioral/psychological way of saying that the weirder someone is, the tougher it's going to be to sell him!

EVEN WEIRDOS BUY

The probability is that some people who buy from you might be in the same category of human behavior as you. Equally predictable is that you will make calls on those who are your behavioral opposite. When we have nothing in common behaviorally with another person it will be more difficult to communicate with them. Just remember that when there is a communications gap between a salesperson and a prospect, it is the salesperson's responsibility to close the gap.

It is incumbent upon us to learn the dynamics of behavioral styles and how to sell different people with different approaches. What the sales profession is about is writing business, not looking for people like ourselves. The fact that a customer's behavioral style is different from yours shouldn't matter if the customer needs, wants, and can buy your product or service. You must learn to understand and deal with behavioral differences in order to achieve your goal of making the sale. We should not be judgmental about other people's behavior; we should be observant of other's behavior so we can learn from it and adapt accordingly.

THREE BEHAVIORAL DIMENSIONS

To get a solid handle on human behavior in selling, let's look at the three basic dimensions of human behavior customarily measured to establish one's behavioral style. They are assertiveness, responsiveness, and adaptability.

Let's define "assertiveness" first by considering the following model outlining characteristics:

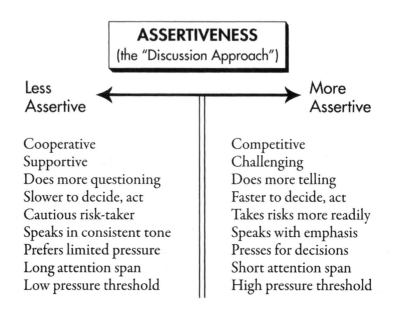

ASSERTIVENESS
(the "Discussion Approach")

Less
Assertive ← ——————— → More
Assertive

Less Assertive	More Assertive
Cooperative	Competitive
Supportive	Challenging
Does more questioning	Does more telling
Slower to decide, act	Faster to decide, act
Cautious risk-taker	Takes risks more readily
Speaks in consistent tone	Speaks with emphasis
Prefers limited pressure	Presses for decisions
Long attention span	Short attention span
Low pressure threshold	High pressure threshold

Definition of Assertiveness: The predictable technique for exchanging information and influencing others.

NOTE: Both more assertive and less assertive types have active approaches to controlling conversations and influencing others' points of view. While these approaches are different, they can both be very effective in selling, managing, parenting, etc.

Study (even memorize!) the assertiveness characteristics. If you learn these and evaluate your prospective buyers according to which extreme their observable behavior tends to lean toward, you will be on your way to understanding prospective buyers better than ever.

The next important dimension of human behavior to study and thoroughly understand is responsiveness.

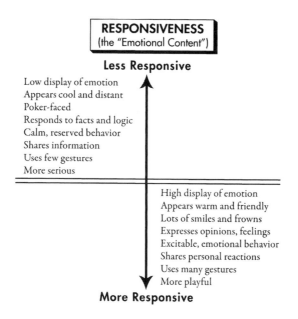

RESPONSIVENESS
(the "Emotional Content")

Less Responsive

Low display of emotion
Appears cool and distant
Poker-faced
Responds to facts and logic
Calm, reserved behavior
Shares information
Uses few gestures
More serious

High display of emotion
Appears warm and friendly
Lots of smiles and frowns
Expresses opinions, feelings
Excitable, emotional behavior
Shares personal reactions
Uses many gestures
More playful

More Responsive

Responsiveness is defined as the extent to which a person reacts, shows feelings and displays emotions.

While heredity and environment both influence current behavior, the people with whom we grew up and the behavior they demonstrated, expected, or praised have contributed to the emotion we have developed the habit of displaying. Verbal and nonverbal responsiveness clues are easy to observe if we pay attention. This information should assist you greatly in developing and utilizing an effective strategy for selling different people differently.

The third principal dimension of human behavior, adaptability, is covered in detail in the next chapter.

OBSERVING HUMAN BEHAVIOR

Now let's look at the bigger picture and discuss how we can profit from paying concentrated attention to the behavior of those people we deal with every day.

We tend not to observe human behavior to the degree that we should. We observe people as a habit, but most of us have not developed observation into a natural and internalized skill. We often react instead, in terms of like or dislike, accept or reject, etc. Reactions of that type aren't productive to us as salespeople. We need to be less reactive and more observant.

Whenever I conduct a seminar, I know that within two minutes after I'm introduced, people are reacting to me—my style, my content, my voice and accent, my mannerisms. Maybe the reaction of some leans toward the positive side of the scale. With others, it may lean toward the negative side. I have to win them over like you do in a sales presentation.

That kind of immediate reaction to another person is normal. But while it is normal, it's not the appropriate response if you intend to become a high performance salesperson. High performers don't react, they observe. Also, the use of exceptional interpersonal skills, humor, and asking thoughtful questions can help immensely.

To learn to observe human behavior we must keep our eyes and ears open. We must tune in to the behavior of others, and we must learn from what we observe. To really learn, it is not enough to just watch and listen. We'll need to take written notes, remember things, categorize, read between the lines, and really study the behavior we have observed.

That's how we'll be able to achieve the other step that's necessary to make observing human behavior productive, and that is to be able to strategize from what we've learned.

Human behavior is observable and verifiable. It's not totally 100 percent black and white, there's always a little gray area. But it's definite enough that we can indeed learn and strategize from it to be more effective with people.

FOUR BEHAVIORAL STYLES

David Merrill defined social style as a particular pattern of actions others observe and agree upon for describing a person's usual behavior.

Merrill and Reid, in their top selling book, *Personal Styles & Effective Performance*, developed an approach that was used effectively within many companies seeking to teach their people more about human behavior and the styles. Dr. Tony Alessandra and I wrote *Selling With Style* further developing the concept of selling different people with different strategies. We have used a variation of these concepts for years now in our sales and management training activities.

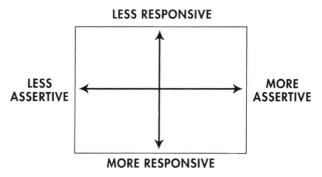

The previous illustration should help you understand the concept of the four behavioral styles. If you combine the horizontal Assertiveness line and the vertical Responsiveness line into the creation of a grid framework, you will find it much easier to quantify and categorize the behavioral styles of your prospects.

Four different combinations of these two behavioral dimensions reveal four distinctly different behavioral styles. Now let's discuss the four resulting behavioral styles.

ANALYTICAL	DRIVER
also known as *Technician or Thinker* *or "HIGH C"*	*also known as* *Dominant or Director* *or "HIGH D"*
Less Assertive, Less Responsive	**More Assertive, Less Responsive**
AMIABLE	EXPRESSIVE
also known as *Relator or Supporter* *or "HIGH S"*	*also known as* *Socializer or Influencer* *or "HIGH I"*
Less Assertive, More Responsive	**More Assertive, More Responsive**

1. DRIVERS

The Driver is the more assertive, less responsive individual, which means that Drivers come on strong with a low display of emotion. At their best, Drivers are task-oriented and achievement-focused. Their short attention span is a motivator to get a lot done in a short period of time, which is another strength. One of the weaknesses of Drivers is that, if they are not careful, they will appear to some as cold, calloused, and unsentimental. They are disciplined about time and reject inaction. A Driver is also known as the Director, the Dominant, the Reserved Teller, or the High D (Dominant).

2. EXPRESSIVES

The Expressive is the more assertive, more responsive type person who comes on strong with a high display of emotion. A strength of Expressives is that they are stimulating, dramatic and goal-focused. At their worst, Expressives may appear to some as loud and disorganized. Expressives like an exciting environment and tend to reject boring, detail-oriented meetings and data. The Expressive is also known as the Socializer, the Influencer, the Emotional Teller, or the High I (Influencer)

3. ANALYTICALS

The Analytical is the less assertive, less responsive type who is laid back and has a low display of emotion. Among the strengths of Analyticals is they are precise and exacting, and they tend to be excellent on detail. At their worst, they will appear to some as boring, picky and dull. The Analytical tends to focus on historical facts and data as their foundation for understanding, and they reject the tendency to shoot from the hip. The Analytical is also known as the Thinker, the Technician, the Reserved Questioner, or the High C (Conscientiousness).

4. AMIABLES

The Amiable is the less assertive, more responsive type who is somewhat laid back but has a high display of emotion. At their best, Amiables are relationship-oriented and will say or do just about anything within reason, short of compromising their integrity, to minimize conflict and get along well with others. At their worst, they come across to some as rather wishy-washy due primarily to their tendency to move slowly on decisions until they understand how everybody feels. The Amiable tends to be an excellent team player and rejects decisive behavior that is insensitive to the feelings of others. The Amiable is also known as the Relater, the Supporter, the Emotional Questioner, or the High S (Steadiness).

WHICH IS BEST, WHICH IS WORSE?

There is no best or worse quadrant in this model, since we all have strengths and we all have weaknesses. It is my opinion that the most successful people in selling and, for that matter, practically any other endeavor, are the men and women who identify their personal strengths and build on them as their foundation for success. They simultaneously identify their human weaknesses, eliminate the ones they can, and at least minimize or manage those they can't totally eliminate. A combination of these strategies increases an individual's effectiveness and performance in dealing with others. Don't fall into the trap of being one who fails because of a functional blindness to your own defects. Equally as important, don't be oblivious to your greatest assets.

So, which of these styles make for the best salesperson? The answer is all of them at one time or another.

Years ago the proverbial "born salesman" was a stereotype comparable to the Expressive style, which was thought to be the best behavioral style for selling. Later, as technology and sophistication grew in all areas, the Analytical's tendency toward accuracy and precision gained favor. This is the stereotype of those often called "Sales Engineers."

Then, when the business world got on a productivity kick a few years ago, Drivers were considered to be among the most successful salespeople. It was thought their result-oriented thrust would bring in more orders. Most recently, with the relationship orientation of business and industry and the high interest in customer service, the Amiable's skills are in the spotlight.

Today it's possible for all of us to be high performance salespeople, regardless of how we're labeled. One of the things about this subject matter is that there's an underlying respect for individuality. You don't have to be just like anyone else. You can learn to be the best you are capable of being by implementing whatever moderate and well-thought-out behavior modifications are needed for maximum effectiveness. A big issue here is your ability to identify the style of your prospect, adapt to that style, and develop a strategy that works best with each prospect.

Regardless of which description you key in on when formulating your high performance sales strategies, it's important to keep the behavioral styles in mind. Salespeople who try to sell everyone the same way will simply suffer unnecessary stress and a low conversion rate of prospects to buyers.

> **People are different. We all have behavioral idiosyncrasies, but we each have a predictable behavioral style. The salesperson's job is not to be judgmental but to get orders from all types. Respect a prospect's individuality and figure out where they are coming from psychologically before trying to sell them.**

Priceless

CHAPTER EIGHT

Adapting to Your Customer

"If my biggest customer tells me to go to hell, I'm going home to pack!"

CAVETT ROBERT

THE SKILL OF ADAPTABILITY

It is clear from our previous chapter the obvious respect that experts have for each of the behavioral styles. It's important to remember that anyone from any of the four styles—the Driver, the Expressive, the Analytical, or the Amiable—can be a high-performance salesperson if they develop the appropriate skills for adapting to others.

In this chapter, we'll deal principally with our willingness and ability to adapt to the styles of our customers. No skill is more important for the high-performance salesperson than adaptability. Adaptability is critical for two reasons: one, you will sell more, and two, it is simply the right thing for people who respect others to do.

To be effective and successful in the selling process, we must adapt to our prospect's style, to their level of understanding, and to the subject matter and areas of focus in which they have the greatest interest and need. Being versatile and flexible and interacting with people can make all the difference in getting results. This also plays well to understanding *what* they value.

DEFINING ADAPTABILITY

Adaptability is an effort to connect and resonate with more people while keeping your own objectives intact. It is being resourceful in varying your methods to be understood and accepted. It's balancing your concern for self, others, and the task at hand with a willingness to step out of your own comfort zone. Synonyms for adaptability are flexibility and versatility. Since we are all creatures of habit, this can be a challenge to learn, but the payoff is significant.

Adaptability is a learnable skill, and it's a skill high-performance salespeople have often perfected, whether knowingly or unknowingly. They've internalized it, and it works for them. For many high performers, it's a natural and spontaneous thing. They've learned how to get to where they need to be in their behavioral mode in order to get on target with the other person.

You've heard about stimulus response, right? You are the stimulus, and you will evoke a positive response if you are the appropriate stimulus. Salespeople in a highly adaptable mode prove to be a positive stimulus. Salespeople who are not very adaptable are simply a negative stimulus and customarily get poorer results from their rigid selling style.

FOLLOW THE RULES

People who are highly adaptable in the selling process are the people who are knowledgeable about, embrace, and practice what is known as the Platinum Rule.

We all know the Golden Rule is, *"Do unto others as you'd have them do unto you."* You can't refute that.

The Platinum Rule is a beautifully simple, valuable concept that says *"Do unto others as they like to be done unto."* We recommend you adopt the Platinum Rule in addition to the Golden Rule. Following the Platinum Rule will enable you to improve your sales results, improve relationships, and become more attuned to the goals of your prospective buyer.

Low adaptability people are not versatile. They are "me-oriented." The focus in their sales presentation is me... me, I... I, us... us. "Look what I've got, see what we've got," they will say. Their self-centered focus turns off prospective buyers. High-performance salespeople focus on the prospective buyer. They are "you" oriented.

My friend, mentor, and a highly successful salesman in the insurance industry, the late Charlie "Tremendous"

Jones used to say, "Selling is identification. If I can identify with you, we can interact for only a few minutes and have a meaningful exchange. If I can't identify with you, we can talk all day and won't say anything to each other."

If you think that becoming highly adaptable takes a lot of work, you're right. The thing that will work in your favor is that you can start now, using the experience and the skills you already have. Work to become more adaptable and you'll see results quickly.

COMPONENTS OF ADAPTABILITY

There are four components of adaptability that we need to understand if we're going to make this skill a natural reflexive skill. Let's look at each of the components more closely:

- IMAGE. An individual's or an organization's image is not a constant, it's an ever-changing variable. Your image is made up of five things: how you look, what you say, how you say it, what you do, and how you do it.

- PRESENTATION. Presentation, in this case, means how you tell your story. Key questions should be answered here: Is your presentation targeted? Is it appropriate in every way? Does it reflect your knowledge of their needs? And, most importantly, is it preceded by a needs analysis?

- COMPETENCE. Competence relates to knowledge of the subject at hand and how to deal with it. I learned many years ago that your breadth of competence will either turn people on or turn them off in short order. In today's competitive marketplace, people want to do business with a pro. They are intolerant of uninformed salespeople and simply won't waste their time on them. Expand your knowledge and competence far beyond your competitor's and you will enjoy a nice edge.

- FEEDBACK. Your willingness and ability to constructively and positively give and receive feedback is a vital part of your communications expertise. Be eager to gain ideas from prospects and clients on how to be better. Ask them for feedback, and listen carefully to their response. When giving feedback to others, do so constructively and sensitively, not critically.

SELLING STRATEGICALLY

To give an effective, adaptable and results-oriented presentation, you need to think in terms of keeping tension and stress low, and keeping trust and credibility high. This will enhance your prospect's comfort level.

A first step toward making your prospect comfortable is to identify his or her behavioral style. If you can then master the skill of selling people the way they like to be sold, your production will skyrocket. Here are some specific strategies that can help you accomplish that.

- With the DRIVER, get to the point. A minimal amount of rapport building is required. Remember that the Driver tends to be the direct, dominant type with a low display of emotion. Drivers reject inaction and respond to an efficient presentation.

- With an EXPRESSIVE, show some enthusiasm and excitement. The Expressive will get excited with you if you appeal to their visions and goals in a stimulating manner. A preponderance of paperwork, complex forms, etc. will be counterproductive with Expressives.

- With an ANALYTICAL, be detailed and specific. If you aren't accurate with an Analytical, you will destroy your credibility. The Analytical wants back-up in the form of spec sheets, computer print-outs, etc. Get overly enthusiastic with an Analytical, deprive them of the data they require, and you'll never sell them. Take your time with them or your efforts just won't work.

- With AMIABLES, be warm and friendly. Keep the peace with the Amiable; don't ask them for the order until you have earned the right through relationship building. Take time to earn his or her trust and you will increase the probability of enjoying a long-term, mutually beneficial relationship with an Amiable.

THE ADAPTABLE SALESPERSON GAINS ALLEGIANCE

Here's a likely prediction for your future in professional selling: You will never again be in a position to take for granted the allegiance of your prospects or customers. Never. Not at any time in your entire sales career. As competition gets tougher, gaining and maintaining allegiance becomes more important. Here's a lesson I learned the hard way.

I worked my way through Memphis State University (now the University of Memphis) selling. Back in those days, most of us took classes in the morning and worked in the afternoons or evenings. I was selling real estate, and the only training I had received was some early courses in the school of hard knocks. It was during this time that I learned to never presume the allegiance of prospects or customers.

During those years, a group of us usually got together for lunch in the student center. One of the students in our group was a nice guy named Tom, whom I got to know fairly well. Over a period of a few months I guess I shared the lunch table with Tom maybe two or three days every week.

One day Tom wasn't there and someone in the group mentioned that he was probably busy. "I understand Tom and his wife just bought a home," my lunch companion said.

My ears perked up and probably turned red, too, like my face. Here I am, a young, hard-working real estate agent, supposedly eager to succeed. I've been looking for prospects, and they tell me Tom has just bought a house, and I knew nothing about it! This was frustrating for me, as you can imagine.

Well, I did a little research and found out that Tom and his wife bought a home from a competitor of mine in the part of town where I specialized. And they could have bought that same house from me. Here I am, having lunch two or three days a week with the guy. I thought we had become pretty good friends, and he buys from someone else. Unbelievable!

For a couple of weeks, I didn't say anything about it. Finally one day, Tom and I were sitting at lunch once again, and I mustered the courage to mention the situation. I didn't want to seem angry or upset. I just wanted to find out what went on inside this guy's head that he would go out and buy from my competitor.

I said, "Tom, I understand you bought a new home recently." Well, he got excited and started telling me all about his new home. I had tremendous difficulty sharing his enthusiasm. But I managed to smile through his descriptions. "It sounds like a great place, Tom," I said. "By the way, I know the builder who built your new house. In fact, I know the house. You're going to like it there, and I'm really happy for you."

Then I said, "But you know, Tom, I've got to tell you that I'm a little frustrated. I am in the real estate business. I sell homes. In fact, I specialize in that particular part of town where you bought. I could have sold you that very same home."

I will never forget as long as I live the response I got. Tom looked at me a few seconds, snapped his fingers, pointed squarely at me with a surprised but serious look on his face and said, "That's right, Hutson! You are in the real estate business, aren't you?" It seems he had temporarily forgotten.

That happened decades ago, and I remember it just like it was yesterday. I didn't make that sale, and I didn't deserve to. Why? I hadn't told Tom, or I hadn't told him enough, or I hadn't told him in the right way, that when he was ready to look for a home, I was ready to help him. I had done nothing to nurture the professional side of the relationship. I hadn't earned the allegiance or the right to that sale.

That was a great lesson for me to learn at that time. You can never, ever take allegiance for granted. It doesn't matter if you have lunch with someone every day. It doesn't matter the degree of the relationship. If you're taking allegiance for granted, you're going to get blindsided.

APPRECIATE PEOPLE'S DIFFERENCES

Another word for adaptability is flexibility. In the context of selling, we should understand that our goal is to be able to sell different people differently. We need to be respectful and flexible in dealing with others to make headway in the relationship-building process. This is a critical part of the behavioral style content to master since, in my opinion, there is a direct correlation between adaptability skills and sales expertise. You need to respect and deal with the individuality of others and sell them in a manner that is comfortable for them.

So if adaptability is your "flexibility tendency", how do you go about learning the skill, internalizing it, and increasing sales with it? Your mission is respecting their agenda without compromising your own goals. Here are the key takeaways regarding adaptability that I would ask you to accept:

1. An attitude that demonstrates that you are willing to adapt will be your foundation of success in this skill.

2. An aptitude that demonstrates that you have the skill to adapt will be the thing that can take you to the next level.

3. You need to clearly understand what adaptability is and how to use it.

4. The effectiveness of your adaptability skills will be predicated on the accurate identification of the person's style.

5. To get your desired outcomes you need to know the strategy that works best with those in each of the four quadrants.

Here's how we can help you discover how you can make adaptability work for you as a sales professional. During your sales process we should utilize adaptable behavior with our prospects. Remember, in selling it is YOUR job to close any communication gaps!

THE ADAPTABILITY CONTINUUM

Regardless of the quadrant you are in on that grid, if you are going to effectively interact with other people you need to understand how to adapt. If you are adaptable you are more likely to help people feel important and make them want to do business with you. We identify low adaptability people as "me-oriented" and preoccupied with their own agenda while the "you-oriented" highly adaptable sales-people are concerned with the agenda of other people.

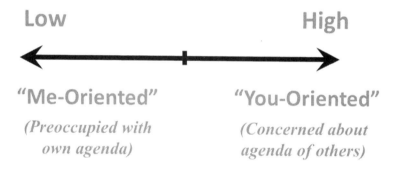

The Adaptability Continuum

Low   High

"Me-Oriented"   **"You-Oriented"**

(Preoccupied with   *(Concerned about*
own agenda)   *agenda of others)*

IDENTIFYING THE "STYLE" OF OTHERS

The successful use of the skills we have been discussing in previous chapters are all predicated on your ability to effectively identify the behavioral style of others. Some are easy and some are challenging, but it is worth the effort to learn and use these skills. In this segment we will teach you what to look for in the style ID process so that you can, with some degree of accuracy, figure out which quadrant someone is in. Here are five guidelines for you to consider to become skilled at identifying the style of others:

1. There is a need to be keenly observant of the behavior of others.

2. You want to both watch and listen carefully to them; remember behavior is what we see and hear people say and do.

3. You will need to simultaneously consider what their assertiveness factor is, and what their responsiveness factor is.

4. Observe not only what they say, but how they say it. It will help to consider their attention span and vocal intensity.

5. Try to become skilled at ascertaining someone's age. If you know which generation they are a part of you will be able to adapt more readily to them and their needs.

If others in your company are involved in this course of study get with them to discuss certain high visibility people you both know. Discuss their style, and more specifically, their assertiveness and responsiveness measures, and you will advance your results in style identification. Now let's go into eight things to look for to help you identify style.

1. Moderate stress tends to clarify style. We become more like we already are when under stress—one's style becomes more apparent.

2. Don't stereotype people into occupational slots. All CPAs are not Analyticals, and all salespeople are not Expressives.

3. Take your time—observe them over time for best results in Style ID when you can.

4. Observe them in multiple settings when possible.

5. Assess whether or not they usually seem in a hurry; that correlates with more assertive behavior.

6. Are they deliberative on details? That is most common among less responsive types.

7. Are they talkative? That behavior is expected of more responsive people.

8. Are they predominantly asking questions? If so, there's a good chance this is a less assertive person.

YOU ARE WHAT YOU WERE WHEN

My friend and colleague, Dr. Morris Massey, used to do a program entitled "You Are What You Were When." His key idea is that when you were born determined many elements of your value system, your beliefs, and ultimately, your behavior. He was way ahead of his time with that concept, but right on point. What we experienced when growing up influenced what we believe and who we became.

Focusing on generational theory is an attempt to find and to understand the characteristics of people according to their birth generation. These studies and information are helpful generalizations. The actual time line and definitions of each of the generations is not a formal or hard science, but rather has been defined by research of popular culture, media, and market research reports.

This concept of generational dynamics became clearly evident as the result of research done on the specific age groups that emerged and developed after the Second World War. The war and its residual effects significantly impacted the value systems of our grandparents, and ultimately their children. The core value systems continue to morph and transition as they impacted and influenced the economy, lifestyle preferences and of course, the global reach of the internet.

As of today, unlike any other time in our history, we have four different generations in the workforce working side by side, each influenced by the values and preferences of the time they were born. These differences add another layer of diversity to how we connect, communicate and ultimately serve each distinct group in ways that resonate with what they want, when they want it and how they choose to be communicated with.

Today, there are multiple studies and much research on the "Four Generations" and how they differ, especially in the workplace, which is what interests us here.

Like the behavioral styles, we need to understand the differences in people based on their generational preferences to better understand and connect with them. When we do our homework, we are in a better position to develop successful strategies for dealing with each. In Sales, it is necessary for each of us to learn how to sell people the way they like to be sold. This section is designed to help you understand the generations, and what you need to know about each to be effective communicators with them.

FOUR GENERATIONS TO UNDERSTAND

Like the previously studied behavioral styles, the four generations content is a "Soft Science" in that not every characteristic described here precisely reflects every individual within each of the generations. The good news is that there are very helpful guidelines even though people develop and maintain their own core values and preferences built on their personal experiences. Members of each of the generational groups share values, experiences and tendencies with those they associated with as they grew up.

So the generational dynamics we are about to get into are applications of the behavior of the four groups that can help us know them better and communicate with them in ways that resonate with their value systems in a more receptive manner.

Well known researcher, John Ansbach says "When we use systems, tools and strategies that resonate with each group's core value and communication preferences, we are able to bridge the communication gaps to help more people with our services and sales solutions."

These insights will prove helpful in crafting the proper interpersonal strategies with people in each of the generations. If we know what their values are it will be easier to connect and understand how to meet their needs which paves the way for a better trust level.

If you know yourself and your own values and learn the values of the other generations, you will be postured to manage relationships with greater expertise and probability of success. The four generations with their descriptors are:

CIVICS: The Civics, aka pre-boomers, were born before 1946 and are generally considered traditionalists. They have been referred to as the "greatest generation" who number over sixty million. They were raised by parents who suffered the effects of the war and the Great Depression. The influence impacted their spending habits, their attitudes towards authority, work ethic and family values. In general, due to these meager times, many people in this age group experienced hardships in their early years which were followed by good times and growing prosperity. They value patriotism and respect. To best resonate with this segment here are tips to get you started on the right foot;

- Be on time (this is also a preference for DRIVER personality styles).

- Be professional in your dress and presentation.

- Don't assume they are not tech savvy, as this is the largest demographic using Facebook, although they are not extensively tech savvy on other online channels.

BOOMERS: The Boomers, born from 1946 to 1964, were impacted by a prosperous economy that occurred after the war. Their core values include dedication to their business, hard work, stability, security and respect for authority. They are sometimes referred to as the "Me Generation".

Boomers were influenced by civil rights, the Vietnam War, the sexual revolution, and space travel, endured high divorce rates, and have pursued the American dream they have heard about all their lives. Some were the radicals of the seventies and the yuppies of the eighties. They have typically been early adopters of new technology and buy more Apple products than any other group because they can afford them. Numbering over eighty million, their core value includes "winning" and the power of team work.

To connect with boomers:

- Approach the sales process as a team effort to help them reach their objectives.

- Implement the "authorship" principle and allow them to be a part of the process.

GEN X: Those in the Generation X group were born from 1965 to 1980 and are about fifty million in number. This group is often labeled the "latchkey kids" due to the influence of two working parents and being home alone. They saw their boomer parents working hard to accumulate the "good things in life" and have a different view from their parents quest for big homes, big toys in contrast to the harsh and frugal issues their parents dealt with. In terms of their values and preferences they don't mind working, but don't have the "loyalty factor" to a company unless it serves their objectives. They often are reticent to invest in a job long term due to their quest for finding "meaningful" work. Although they are focused on themselves, they are interested in their communities and offer strong support and attention to community efforts, and are the largest online supporters of charities. They are into fun, diversity, education, informality, life balance, personal gratification, and are in general fiercely independent. It has been speculated that they will be the first generation in America that will not do as well financially as their parents did.

To connect with GenXer's here are a few engagement tips:

- GenX prefers a workplace that is fun and inspiring. This may require some flexibility on the corporate limitations to their workspace. Be receptive to allowing their creativity and personalization to come through.

- The GenXers are very self-reliant—micro-management is not appreciated.

- They prefer a more informal work environment both from interactions and for attire.

- This generation seeks out balance between work and personal life. GenX is open to more flexible work hours and work structure, as they will deliver on time, but at their own pace.

MILLENNIALS: Millennials (also known as Generation Y) are the demographic that follow Generation X. Wikipedia reports that although "there are no precise dates when the generation starts and ends their birth dates generally range from the 1980's to the year 2000."

They were influenced by digital media, school shootings, terrorist acts, and came of age in times of economic expansion. They grew up more sheltered than any other generation, and they hope to be the next great generation and turn around the wrongs they have witnessed in the world. In terms of values and preferences, they tend to be confident, techno-focused, moral, civic-minded and collaborative. They also appreciate achievement, extreme fun, high morals, tolerance, enjoy personal attention, tend to be optimistic, are highly competitive, and feel they are members of the global community.

To best connect with the Millennial Generation, here are a few tips:

- They prefer to engage at their own option.

- Millennials tend to communicate using a specific medium of their choosing, and have proven to be heavy users of text messaging, considering email passé.

- This age group prefers to be mentored, not trained, and enjoy the leadership of the mentoring process.

PROCESSING AND ACTING ON THIS INFORMATION

Each generation has its own idiosyncrasies and differences and it is up to us to sort out how each group prefers to be communicated with. As we sort out their unique set of core values, and understand the events that influenced them, we can start to understand their preferences. As we continue to attempt to close communication gaps and get on target with the people we attempt to do business with, this information can be extremely valuable to each of us. If we know our customers better than those we compete with we are provided with an excellent opportunity to create relationship differentiation.

Adaptability Tips:

- Civics: To communicate with the Civics, use discretion and present your story in a logical, somewhat formal manner. Respect their age and use proper grammar. Deliver your message on the traditions of your company and how the solution you are presenting can be a good fit for them.

  Keys to working with the Civics are an understanding that work is not necessarily fun, and that it is important to follow traditional rules. They get frustrated when they observe a lack of discipline and they want you to consider their feelings during the interchange. They like a service-oriented personal touch.

- Boomers: To communicate with the Boomers, remember that they like a diplomatic, direct approach with flexible options. Answer their questions thoroughly and expect to be pressed for details from time to time. Include them in your consensus building activities or they may be offended. First names are okay, and they like a friendly rapport.

Keys to working with the Boomers are that they want to hear that their ideas matter. They want to be valued as they have been all their lives. Silliness and small talk are useless to them and they expect their opinions and feelings to matter. They do well in teams, and are motivated by their responsibilities to others. They don't take criticism very well.

- GenX: To communicate with the Gen Xers, it is okay to be direct and even blunt. And stay in the immediate time frame. Use straight talk and present facts and details in a credible manner. Share info from the start and short sound bites are fine. Don't attempt to micro-manage them and for best results tie your message to results.

Keys to working with the Gen Xers are they realize that they value their independence in the workplace and like to take advantage of options for informality. They want time to pursue their own interests, not just yours. They have a need for the latest technology and want to have fun.

- GenY/Millennials: To communicate with the Millennials (Ys), be polite, respectful, positive, and motivational in your approach. They like electronic communications best, but know the importance of in-person communications on important messages. Show them respect and they will respect you. They will resent criticism or someone talking down to them.

Keys to working with the Millennials are participating in a team-oriented type decision, realizing they want to work with bright and creative people. They were raised to feel positive about themselves and want you to respect that. They like to work with friends and enjoy engaging experiences. They expect rewards for extra effort and excellence.

Internalizing the skill of adaptability with the different generations is training time well spent. Your just rewards are on the way when you please people by communicating with them in the manner they prefer. They recognize your efforts and appreciate them.

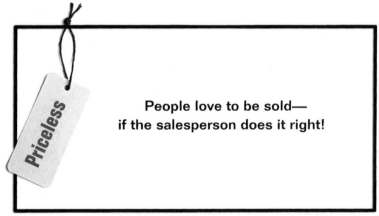

**People love to be sold—
if the salesperson does it right!**

Priceless

CHAPTER NINE

Understanding
Their Needs

"In selling like in medicine, prescription before diagnosis is malpractice."

JIM CATHCART

In the profession of selling today, the diagnosis stage is the process of performing an in-depth needs analysis. Today performing a comprehensive needs analysis is a more important step in the selling process than ever before. Asking the right questions is like an X-ray into the cortex, their human computer.

You can do a better job for your customers, your company and yourself if you'll perform a needs analysis with each sales effort. All other things being equal, the salesperson who can competently perform a needs analysis will enjoy a significantly higher conversion percentage than salespeople who cannot or do not. The salesperson today who makes a presentation without first performing a needs analysis is simply stacking the cards against himself.

Years ago, the selling process often evolved into a debate. The salesperson who had more answers than the prospect had objections often made the sale. Today, a win-win attitude is favored and, as time goes by, will become even more important. Confrontational, debate-oriented sales approaches are a thing of the past. They are not conducive to making a sale today or developing relationships for making future sales.

OBJECTION-FREE SELLING?

When salespeople are involved in needs-analysis selling that is done properly, they experience something that often amazes them. The number of sales objections they experience will customarily drop dramatically.

One reason this occurs is that you have uncovered the prospect's true feelings, apprehensions, desires, needs and what they value so well that negative input in the selling cycle is less likely.

Needs-analysis selling puts you in a position of making higher quality recommendations and thus doing a superior job for your customer. It shows your customers that you are genuinely interested in them and the results they gain. The customer is far more comfortable with this approach because they see you as a professional problem solver who is a valuable resource, rather than a shallow persuader who just wants another sale.

Give yourself a competitive edge. Vow today to become one of the best in your field at needs-analysis selling.

NEEDS ANALYSIS DEFINED

What is needs analysis selling? It's a process of information-gathering performed to help you discover customers' wants, needs and what they most value, followed by in-depth examination of all factors that impact the buying decision.

Your goals in performing a needs analysis should be:

1. To create initial positive prospect involvement (a means of winning the prospect over early).

2. For you and the prospect to become keenly aware of, and begin to focus on, existing needs and desires. You will ultimately want to uncover their dominant buying motive and, of course, the things they truly value.

3. For you to gain a clear assessment and understanding of those needs as the prospect sees them. When there are multiple needs, attempt to ascertain the priority the prospect assigns to them. You will now start to understand what they value most.

4. For you to establish genuine trust and rapport with the decision makers and the decision

influencers as you gain an authentic understanding of their feelings and desires.

5. To gain sufficient high-quality input so that
you are positioned for an affirmative decision
when you make your recommendations.

LET'S GET STARTED

Now let's get into the process. First a question: Did you
ever hear of a salesperson who gave an absolutely magnificent sales presentation to someone who could not make a
decision? I bet we've all done that at some juncture in our
selling career.

Work diligently to try to talk with every person whose
opinion will impact the ultimate decision. That might well
include not only principal decision makers, but also users
of the product or service or people on the periphery who
might well be decision influencers. Even if your interaction with these people is brief, remember: The more people whose opinion you ask, the more you will learn and the
more allies you will have an opportunity to create within
that organization. This will facilitate your attempt to make
the sale, and it will be very helpful in subsequent sales calls
on that organization. People enjoy being given opportunities for authorship!

You need to understand their "DMU" (Decision
Making Unit). If you know each person in the DMU,
their position, and their wants and needs, you are on your
way to a YES.

In a good needs-analysis setting, studies indicate that early on you should do 20 percent or less of the talking and your prospect or prospects should do 80 percent or more. Remember, the needs analysis is an information-gathering process and it's smart to take in-depth notes.

THE PALEST INK...

You may have heard it said that "the palest ink is better than the greatest memory." One activity that impresses prospective buyers is to reference specific details, quotes or facts that you learned from them in a previous visit. It shows them that you are a pro, a good record keeper, a person concerned about the details related to their needs, someone who is concerned about helping them make quality decisions based on thorough information gathering. It also serves to remind them that no interaction with you is a waste of time.

Memory experts say we forget 64 percent of what we hear within 24 hours, and 96 percent within 15 days. Based on the interim period between sales calls, if we don't take diligent notes, we can turn prospective buyers off with our inability to capture, store and reference important data from previous appointments.

One good reason for taking lots of notes is the high-impact and positive impression it makes on the prospect. People love to see you write down what they say. The prospect will be impressed when you say, "Mr./Mrs. Martin, you may recall that on November 2 you told me that your loss-claim ratio was approximately two percent...is that still the case?" Don't rely on your memory, take notes and save those brain cells for amassing new skills.

Whether you are talking to a group of people in a needs-analysis setting or interviewing numerous people individually, it is recommended you put the initials of the individual in front of the notes you take so you will know who said what. This can be very important to you later when evaluating all the information.

GATHERING INFORMATION FROM THE MASSES

Many times you will find that several people will be involved in the needs- analysis process.

Most people would agree that all of us are smarter than one of us. And many times a great synergism can be created. Remember that high-performance salespeople always assess needs before selling products and services. That's another code which should never be violated.

The length of time spent on a needs analysis can vary widely. If you sell a high-ticket item, the needs analysis might require several visits with numerous people over an extended period of time. On the other hand, if you're selling a low ticket item or product, you might make a call, do a brief needs analysis, and give your presentation and recommendations in one call.

In any selling scenario, the needs analysis, even if brief, will contribute greatly to your sales results. Here are some helpful guidelines you can use in performing your needs analysis:

1. Do more listening and writing than talking. Remember; try to do 20% or less of the talking in this phase of the sales process.

2. Try to get pertinent in-depth information. Get below the surface issues if you can. You may need to assure your prospect that the information will be kept confidential.

3. Ascertain what kind of solution they have used in the past for similar problems and needs, since the best predictor of future behavior is past behavior. This will help you know your prospect better, the company's buying behavior, and perhaps influence your recommendations.

4. Learn their company philosophy, goals and mission when you can, and learn who the key players are. That will normally be very helpful later.

5. Always end your needs analysis with a general question. Try something like: "Is there anything I haven't asked you today that would be important for me to know at this point?" This is general, but it often ends the needs analysis session on a high note with a good interaction.

THE 36,000-FOOT NEEDS ANALYSIS

Meeting a stranger on an airplane and ultimately selling him my service is a gratifying experience. I've done this on numerous occasions through the years after conversing with an interesting executive at a high altitude.

A few years ago on a non-stop flight from Memphis to San Francisco I met Charles Sebastian, a distinguished executive and President and CEO of Aerojet Tactical Corporation. This was my first (and only!) encounter with someone in the business of manufacturing rockets.

We exchanged pleasantries, began talking, and soon he had invited me to call him "Chuck." As we continued to talk, I sensed some frustration on his part, despite his upbeat professional style.

More evidence of Chuck's frustration came to the surface as he began explaining that he had been with Aerojet for about 20 years but president for only six months. The company's dozen or so senior vice presidents were doing a good job, he went on to say, but several of them were disappointed that they did not get the nod for the presidency. (Chuck had been an Aerojet senior vice president himself before being named president.)

As he elaborated, I learned that the morale in the upper ranks of their organization was not up to par, despite Chuck's diligent efforts as the company's new leader to win the senior vice presidents over after the transition. After discussing some of the problematical aspects of this situation in depth, Chuck turned to me and asked, "What business are you in?" I replied, "I am a speaker, author, and consultant to corporations."

"You are? Well perhaps you would have some ideas on how I can deal with this dilemma," he said.

"Chuck," I replied, "I do have some ideas on it, but if we are going to look into your situation in greater depth, I would like to do it right. Is it okay if I take some notes?"

He approved and with that, I got my briefcase out from under the airline seat, pulled a legal pad from it, and proceeded to begin my needs analysis process. "Let's start from the beginning," I said.

At those words, Chuck eagerly jumped in and began providing detailed information for me as I furiously took notes. Remembering that in a good needs analysis session the salesperson should do less than 20 percent of the talking, I made my questions brief and direct. In the best case scenario, the customer or prospect will take the lead and start giving in-depth responses. Fortunately, that's what Chuck did.

He appreciated seeing me taking notes. In fact, he looked over my shoulder quite often to observe what I was writing down. In one case, he even leaned over closer and pointed to the pad, saying, "You misspelled that name right there." He was really into it! An hour and forty-five minutes—and several pages of handwritten notes—later, the bell sounded that signaled our descent into San Francisco.

I decided it was time for a trial question, so I said, "Chuck, as I understand it, what you would like me to do is consider this information and put together a proposal of the best solution to the problem from a training point of view."

"That's right," he said. "If you could get something to me in a couple of weeks, that would be great."

I said that would be fine but, I added, "If it's okay with you, Chuck, I may need to call you back on a couple of occasions to gather more information and perhaps talk with some of your senior vice presidents. Would that be OK?" Chuck agreed.

I sent him my press kit and references when I returned to Memphis, and by then I was into program development.

Chuck and I talked on the telephone on two or three occasions during the following week to discuss minor details of the training assignment. I also had conversations with some of their key people. I then put together and FedExed him a comprehensive proposal representing a substantial corporate training package for Aerojet. Chuck liked what he saw and he bought it.

I am convinced that Chuck signed that contract, not because I was a great salesperson, but because I did an excellent job of gathering information and then presented to him a solution which he helped create.

WINNING WITH NEEDS ANALYSIS

The professionally performed needs analysis by experienced sales pros is a thing of beauty. When done well it sets a salesperson apart quicker than anything else. Prospects love it because the focus is on them, rather than your product or service. That conversation needs to come later. Performing an in-depth needs analysis, with excellent questions and a genuine concern for them, is what earns you the right to ultimately tell your story and ask for their business!

Any salesperson who gives a sales presentation without asking needs-analysis questions first, is not a professional.

There might be one critical item of information you gather in a needs analysis that is the very thing that ultimately makes the difference between a made sale and a lost sale. You must know their true wants, needs and value points to hit the bull's eye with your solution.

The best way to perform a professional needs analysis is to adhere to the most critical principles. Here are six important ones:

1. Ask permission to ask them questions—An example might be: "I'm excited about sharing ideas with you regarding our options and deliverables, but first I need to ask you some questions to better understand your needs. Is that okay?"

2. Seek their engagement. As soon as you begin asking them questions and showing considerable interest in them, they will be more compelled to openly share important information with you.

3. Be well prepared to take notes either on a legal pad or your iPad. They will love watching you write down what they say. It shows you are interested and demonstrates that you are going through the process properly. Remember too,

that you will retain much more about them and their needs when taking thorough notes.

4. Ask great questions. Ask questions that are better than the shallow ones everybody else asks. The better the question, the better and more illuminating the answer you get.

5. Ask for elaboration. When you get a yes or no response, a smart move is to probe for more information, you may opt to say, "If you wouldn't mind, I'd like to drill a little deeper on this topic. Could you elaborate on what brought this about?" Many times you will get more valuable information on the elaboration than you did on the initial question.

6. Last, but certainly not least, use the "Authorship Principle" to increase the impact, pertinence, and results of your presentation.

The "Authorship Principle" is all about asking great questions and gathering key elements of critical information. Then and only then will you be able to craft and deliver a sales presentation which your prospect helped you design! That's a presentation, by the way, that has a great chance of getting you a YES.

CREATING THE "WANT TO"

Your prospects are not going to listen carefully to you until they decide they want to. You can help develop this "want to" by building rapport and asking good questions about them and their needs. Get on target with your prospects by conversing as you hold good eye contact, listen intently and take notes to absorb what they tell you about them and what they value.

Good listeners are also skilled at giving positive validating feedback with statements like "That certainly makes sense." Or "I understand why you would feel that way." Or "That explains why your priorities are focused on this area."

Your consultative needs analysis is, in effect, one or more interviews. If you do a credible job of drawing them out and getting them talking it is likely you will succeed in discovering not only their wants, needs, and buying motives, but also their priorities and what they value most.

LET'S DO IT YOUR WAY

When we launched the VT (Virtual Training) Division of U. S. Learning we had a number of clients who had just invested sizable sums of money in their own LMS (Learning Management System). Their first question when looking at our new programs was "Can this be integrated into our LMS?" Our platform partner didn't recommend it since it involved a good bit of labor and some costs for the sake of accessing the program through the client's LMS portal. Our partner tried to talk us out of making that option available. They had no idea how important this was to our clients, so we went to work figuring out the best ways to accomplish this in a customer-friendly manner.

We managed to come up with some good solutions which delighted our clients. The fact that we were willing to figure out how to do it this way meant a lot to them and helped us get more commitments. Sometimes we have to step out of our comfort zones to do what needs to be done to amaze and delight our customers.

VICTIM OF WHAT?

A few years ago I was on the Dean Selection Committee for the College of Business at The University of Memphis. This process took a year and a half and became quite complex. One fellow executive on the committee was rather exasperated in one long meeting and said "I think we need to absolutely require..." then he articulated about five demanding elements that would have made it even harder to find a qualified candidate for the position.

I'll never forget the response of the lead V. P. from the headhunter firm who was on hand for the meeting. He said "I don't think we want to get that stringent in our requirements at this point. We might become victims of our own compulsive rigidity." I never forgot that statement, and I have used it on more than one occasion in business discussions. If we are going to be adaptable we need to be sensitive to the needs of others without being obsessed with our own agenda. My recommendation is be rigid on the discipline we require of ourselves to succeed, but flexible when responding to the needs and agendas of others. We will win more friends and influence more people in the process.

Priceless

If you proficiently perform the needs analysis, you are preparing yourself to ultimately deliver a presentation that your prospects helped design. Do this and you'll sell more, faster than ever before.

CHAPTER TEN

Questioning and Listening Expertise

"None of us can learn anything when we are talking!"

HARVEY MACKAY

ADVANCED QUESTIONING SKILLS

The effective deployment of the questioning process is a skill which, when learned in advanced form, can be a terrific differentiator for salespeople. Our approach here is to give you tips and skills which are superior to those most salespeople tend to use. Years ago selling was about TELL-ING first and foremost, today it is more about ASKING first and telling later. If you do it right, you will probably be doing no more than 20% of the talking in the early part of the interview as we discussed in the needs analysis chapter.

Here are some tips for effective question design for your consideration:

1. Prepare as many of your questions in advance as you can and base them on what you know thus far about the client and their situation.

2. Ask "industry related front-loaded questions" designed to get them talking. An example would be "In light of the improving economy and improved outlook in the oil field, are you going to be carrying bigger parts inventories going forward?" It tells them you've done your homework.

3. Design some "client-centered front-loaded questions" that lets them know that you are up to speed on what's happening in their company. Example: "Since your earnings this quarter beat Wall Street's estimates will that have an impact on your growth strategy?"

4. Use "Open-ended Questions" to get more details from their answers. Many times you will get opinions and feelings in these responses in addition to facts. Example: "How is the economy impacting your dealer network at this time?"

5. Ask "Close-ended Questions" when you want basic information; many times these questions

can be answered with one word. "Are you going to be open on Good Friday?" for example.

6. The "Competitive Leverage Question" is great to ask when you are NOT the current or preferred supplier. You might say: "Ms. Norton, when your existing supplier sat down with you to do your annual review, and vision plan for the coming year, what did they come up with as far as upgrades in products or services for the future?" This type of inquiry makes the assumption of positive behaviors on the part of your competitor which probably DIDN'T EVEN HAPPEN, which will reflect positively on you.

7. Ask "Pain Point Questions" which are designed to gain clarity on the really troublesome issues your prospect is currently dealing with. This should create windows of opportunity for you. Example: "You mentioned new merger activity that has strengthened some of your competitors. How will that impact your sales training activities?"

8. Finally, ask "Impact Questions" which are designed to point out problems and shed positive light on your solutions. An example would be: "What effect will system flaws like the one you just shared, have on your ability to meet your numbers this quarter?"

Now let's talk about the best practices of question deployment. These are the things that will give you a special edge of effectiveness in the questioning process.

1. Work from document (hard copy or computer/tablet based). When they see your comprehensive, well-organized notes and file on their company, they will know you take your research process seriously.

2. Ask only one question at a time, to be sure to cover all aspects of that issue before going to the next. Three part questions don't work well. Those who ask multiple part questions are flawed in their approach.

3. It is usually best to ask fewer questions and cover them thoroughly rather than fire-hosing them with multiple questions and covering them in a shallow manner.

4. Match the question to the person; assuming more than one person is representing their side. It creates involvement of more parties and shows your knowledge of their decision making unit.

5. Probe for more information when necessary; one more short follow-up question will precipitate valuable interchange that you might not have otherwise received.

6. Regularly seek clarification and validation that you are on the right track.

7. Methodically summarize data gathered at the conclusion of the visit, for accuracy and to put it all in context.

8. Remember to have a "Next Steps Discussion" as you approach the conclusion of the interview, to tee things up for follow up.

9. At any juncture in the process that you feel you have received "Buying Signals" indicating it is time to ask for the business, do so.

10. And last but not least, thank them for the opportunity to work with them and for the open interchange of ideas.

HOW TO ASK SENSITIVE QUESTIONS

Your questions about sensitive or personal issues may go unanswered unless you first assure your customer that you'll keep this information in confidence. You might say something like, "Mr./Mrs. Prospect, in order to do the best job possible for you, I need to ask some questions. Some of the questions will be simple and routine, and some may touch on some in-depth or rather confidential areas. Two things are important here. One is that any questions you would rather not answer, just tell me. No problem. Second, please be assured that the information you share with me will not be available to anyone else unless it is a colleague who is assisting me in developing your solution. Is that okay?"

In effect, you are simultaneously doing three valuable things:

1. You're asking their permission to ask questions.

2. You're letting them know that this is a necessary part of the process for best serving him.

3. You're assuring them that their information will be kept in confidence.

This process should reduce any defensiveness or apprehension the prospect may have toward you and it should make him more comfortable with you.

The first question to ask yourself is, "What do we want to learn and why are you asking questions? The answer is, to carry out the information-gathering process in a professional, structured manner and let the prospect know that it is their needs you'll be addressing. In addition, with better information, you are setting yourself up to be in a position to make the highest quality recommendations to them.

Ask an appropriate quantity of questions for openers. Don't overdo it, but be thorough enough to be professional. Simply asking the prospect their opinions can be extremely effective.

ASK QUESTIONS TO HELP YOU GET VALUABLE INFORMATION

I think you'll agree that the toughest person to sell is the one who never says anything. The best solution to engaging this type of person is to get them talking by asking questions. The better the questions you ask, as the higher the quality of the information gathered.

Asking the right questions, at the right time, in the right way, is a true skill that requires diligent practice and pays great dividends. I'm convinced that most of the highest performing salespeople today have mastered this skill and continue to cultivate it in an attempt to perfect it even further.

Here are some quick tips to help you structure better questioning to understand your prospects needs and wants:

- Ask questions that will reveal the prospect's mind-set or position on the topical area. Something as general as "How do you feel about the current delivery times we have discussed?" will usually work well. But assuming that we know how a customer feels about an issue can get us in trouble. Remember that reality is a viewpoint, and their viewpoint may be very different from yours, or most other prospects.

- Ask questions necessary to inform you of what the client wants to accomplish in the subject area. For example: "Mr./Mrs. Prospect, would you tell me about your goals in this area?" Your mission is to ascertain what they value most.

A NEGLECTED SKILL

Have you ever missed a luncheon appointment by going to the wrong restaurant? Or missed meeting someone at the airport because you had the wrong flight information? I have a friend who flew in for a meeting to find he was a day late, and others who found themselves in Hot Springs, Virginia when they were supposed to be in Hot Springs, Arkansas.

What's the central problem behind these scenarios? It is usually due to poor listening skills. It's been said that we receive twelve to fourteen years of training in writing, eight to ten years in reading, six weeks to a year in learning about speaking. But how much training have any of us ever received in listening skills? Not much, unfortunately.

If you're like most of us, you have very little if any instruction in how to listen. And yet, studies say that when you look at the breakdown of how we communicate, you'll find that we spend 9 percent of our time communicating by writing, 16 percent by reading, 30 percent by talking, and 45 percent of our communication takes place by listening. This means you have the least amount of training for the way you communicate most often.

Without good listening skills, we don't understand or remember what was said. If we are going to be truly consultative in our approach, we need to be exceptional listeners. So be an eager learner of these skills to gain an edge.

ACTIVE LISTENING SKILLS

The underlying philosophy of listening is that it is the respectful manner in which you show interest in the agenda of others and learn the most important reasons why they feel the way they feel. We've all also heard that we have two ears and one mouth for an excellent statistical reason! The best sales professionals today are expert listeners, not just articulate presenters. This is in contrast to years ago when everyone attached a special premium to one's ability to deliver an eloquent presentation. Ken Blanchard and I put forth a key axiom in our book, *The One Minute Entrepreneur*, which states that "If you want to succeed with people, lead with your ears!"

Hopefully, by now you have grasped the idea that listening is one of the most important skill sets today's sales professional can possess. It is really difficult for some to develop the skill of asking great questions, then listening intently to the answers. Now let's discuss the impacts of good listening skills.

Active listening is essentially a means of complementing the "passive" process of intently listening, with the "active" behavior of doing several observable things which demonstrate that you are listening and capturing valuable information. Here are seven recommended behaviors to consider:

1. Attach seriousness to the note-taking process. Either write notes on a legal pad or type it into your iPad or laptop as they share ideas with you.

2. Use as much an appropriate level of eye contact as you can while taking the notes.

3. Display occasional nods of agreement or a raised eyebrow, to show you are in tune with them.

4. Offer periodic commentary on major points, like "I'm sure that's more important than ever in this economy", since encouragement stimulates more conversation.

5. Early in the interview, after you have asked for permission to do your needs analysis, adhere to the rule of doing no more than 20% of the talking. Let the time be theirs to express their feelings and agenda. It will be your turn to do more of the talking later. This diagram says it all about who should be talking and when.

THE SALES INTERACTION DYNAMIC

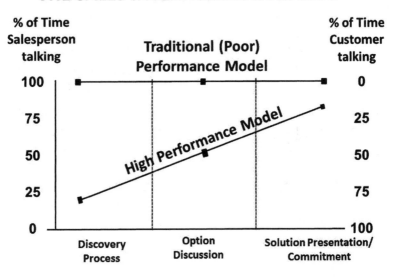

6. As we hear critically important information, show our concern with non-verbal responses.

7. Exceptional needs analysis and listening skills will get more intelligence on the table, giving you the opportunity to create a "wide-angle focus" for considering options and possibilities.

You have, no doubt, heard that knowledge is power! Let's address how we can manage the input and knowledge we are able to secure. There are four levels of our illustration...

- First is DATA which can be numerical or factual.

- The second is INFORMATION—which is what you are able to get from processing the data.

- Third is INTELLIGENCE—which is gained from wisely extrapolating what you can use from information; and finally there is the fourth level...

- WISDOM—which is gained after you have successfully used intelligence to get smart. Asking good questions and listening skillfully will help you get the wisdom you need to be on a success track in selling.

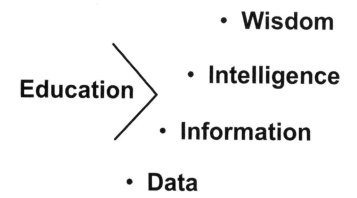

The more skilled we are at listening, the more we learn. As we learn more and process the facts gathered the better chance we have of capturing this wisdom we need to excel. Skilled active listeners can expect five benefits:

- First, you gain enhanced credibility when you show the interest in your prospect that is implied with really good questions and a viable process of listening and observing.

- Second, the questioning and listening process can give you and them a "wide-angle lens" which can result in the consideration of new and exciting solutions and possibilities.

- Third, the better your questioning and listening skills, the more they will talk, enabling you to learn more and get more opportunities to read between the lines for depth and understanding.

- Fourth, skilled listeners are perceived as being more empathetic, advancing the relationship.

- Fifth, good listeners are better at filling "knowledge voids".

SIX STEPS TO BECOMING A GOOD LISTENER

First, good listeners absorb. Poor listeners impatiently wait their turn to speak, thinking about what they'll say next. Listen for understanding, not for designing your response. The best way a salesperson can absorb is to go into an interview with a pre-determined resolve to concentrate on what the prospect says.

Second, good listeners reflect. They reflect what's just been said to acknowledge and ensure their inner thoughts. Or they reflect outwardly or verbally. An example of verbal reflection would be when you say something like, "Mrs. Raines, am I understanding correctly that your senior vice president has mandated securing higher-grade components for overall quality assurance?"

In other words, we rephrase and clarify important points to improve understanding as well as general listening skills. Poor listeners jump in often with a poor bridge to the speaker's previous comments. Instead of reflecting what has just been said, poor listeners turn the focus on themselves.

Third, good listeners respond to what has been said. A general or simple comment in agreement with the speaker's premise is all it takes. Poor listeners often respond with an off-target statement. If this has happened to you, you know how frustrating it can be. Off-target statements often indicate that the listener wasn't, and it really turns prospective buyers off.

Fourth, pay total attention. Concentrate on your prospect's remarks and try to read between the lines to ascertain full meaning. Don't just pretend you're listening to appease your prospect; strive to learn more than your competitor would in the same scenario.

Fifth, be a student of non-verbal skills. People don't always say exactly what they think or feel. Observe gestures, expressions, voice inflections, and special emphasis on key points. Remember, too, that you can usually increase a person's inclination to talk with good eye contact, nods, positive responses, etc., and decrease their verbalizations with a lack of these behaviors.

Sixth, enable venting when the prospect feels the need. Sometimes a prospect gets emotional and must speak out about the strong feelings they have. Let them! Don't interrupt or take issue. Allow them get it all out, and then acknowledge their concerns by responding, "I can understand how you feel..."

QUESTIONING AND LISTENING DURING SALES NEGOTIATIONS

When Dr. George Lucas and I wrote the book, *The One Minute Negotiator*, we had the goal of giving people multiple options to negotiate with others successfully. As you know, the title of this book is Selling Value. The implication is that you need to build value rather than cut price, and I am dedicated to providing multiple skills to help you do this. Most of the content of this book plays to collaborating with prospects and clients with a philosophical approach based on relationship building. Good questioning and listening skills will uncover with greater efficiency the periodic need to negotiate and be of great assistance in deciding what strategy to use.

The reality is, sometimes you need to negotiate in a highly competitive marketplace under conditions which make collaboration near impossible. The key is to develop the skill sets to succeed under any conditions, and this section is designed to help prepare you to do so. I have seen some salespeople who will try harder to get their manager to approve a price cut that they do to get the prospect to buy at the rate card. Our goal is to negotiate with prospects first and see if you can secure a reasonably profitable sale. Negotiation skills are a critical element of the mix if you plan on succeeding long term.

Most experts who have written books and taught negotiation seminars in recent years have focused on Competitive (win-lose) tactics. In our book, we felt we could best teach negotiations with a broader model offering more choices than going to war with each sales opportunity. So we developed a four quadrant "Matrix" to display the strategic choices we have at our disposal in sales negotiations.

The vertical axis of the matrix is about activation. In other words, who initiated this negotiation? The proactive extreme is the top half of the line, representing the initiator, and the reactive extreme is the bottom half of the line where the other person reacts to the negotiation being presented.

The horizontal axis on the matrix is about cooperation. The left half is for low cooperation, and the right half is for high cooperation, resulting in a framework which is shown in the following illustration.

The Negotiation Matrix

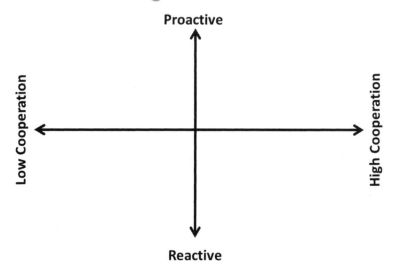

To complete the matrix, there are four distinctly different negotiation strategies formulated by the combination of the two characteristics shown above.

Low Cooperation and Reactive:

The lower left hand quadrant of the matrix is for the people who are low cooperation and reactive. We call this quadrant the **Avoider**. These people either display a reluctance to engage ("Negotiaphobia"), or participate in purposeful avoidance. An example of the latter would be the prospect who suspects your request for an appointment is to discuss a year-end price increase, and he puts you off rather than engage. So many avoiders push back when they already have an acceptable solution in place.

Cooperative and Reactive:

The lower right hand quadrant is for those who are high cooperation and reactive. We call these people the **Accommodator.** They want to be nice and are willing to give something up to show it. Accommodators need to be careful about what they are giving up. Our advice is to know what you are giving up, why you are doing so, and what you hope to get in return. Accommodating does not build relationships, it tests them. One justifiable time to accommodate is when you or your company has made a mistake and you are trying to make amends.

Frankly, not too many great deals get put together on the bottom half of our matrix. When it happens it is the exception rather than the rule.

Low Cooperation and Proactive:

The top left hand quadrant is for those who are low cooperation and proactive. This is the **Competitor**, one who is typically into the win-lose negotiation. They will try to get every morsel on the table they can get. A strong relationship is rarely in place with competitive negotiators. This is the model which historically has most often been taught in negotiation training programs.

High Cooperation and Proactive:

The top right hand quadrant is for those who are high cooperation and proactive, and these are the people who are looking for a win-win, hopefully long term, relationship. There is terrific long-term potential for the **Collaborator**. Just be advised that you can expect to earn every bit of the business you get over time because of the labor and attention required to truly collaborate. The completed matrix is shown in the illustration below.

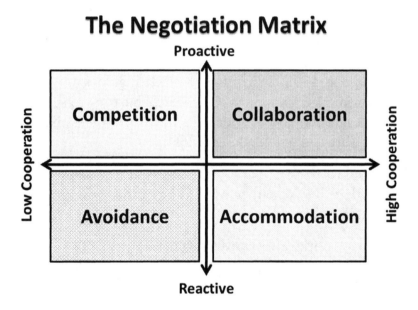

The Negotiation Matrix

Proactive

Low Cooperation	Competition	Collaboration	High Cooperation
	Avoidance	Accommodation	

Reactive

The best negotiators, we have discovered, are the ones who learn all four strategies, can use them well, and know how and when to engage. The internalizing of the skills within this model will help those with "Negotiaphobia" not only cope more successfully, but negotiate with more confidence and with more positive results.

Obviously, you need to communicate well with any potential customer, regardless of the quadrant we find them in initially, but the more you move them toward collaboration, the more important our questioning and listening skills are and the more time you will need to devote to them.

The illustration below shows the importance of, and time which should be devoted to questioning and listening skills with each quadrant.

QUESTIONING AND LISTENING IN SALES NEGOTIATIONS

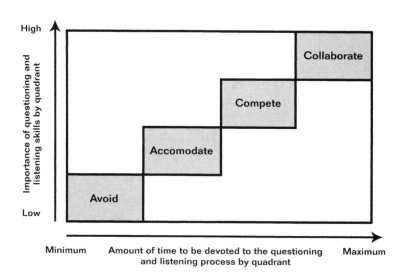

Here's my tip on using the Compromise tactic we hear so much about today. It is terribly misused by most people who are involved in negotiations. We define it as a tactic which is based on seeking an agreement by splitting the difference between two parties' positions. If you want compromise to work for you, there are three provisos that are important:

1. It should only be used late in a negotiation.

2. When there is a small gap in parties' positions.

3. And based on confirmed resolution.

> **Priceless**
>
> Converse with as many decision influencers as possible. Ask quality questions with great skill. Listen attentively and respond with thoughtful reflection. Take diligent notes. When needed, probe further for detail, depth of feelings, and opinions. Clarify and confirm often to avoid misunderstandings. Negotiate thoughtfully and never forget the reason you have two ears and one mouth!

PART IV

SECURING AND GROWING THE BUSINESS

CHAPTER ELEVEN

Establishing the Value of Your Solution

"It's easier to explain price once than to apologize for quality forever."

ZIG ZIGLAR

TODAY'S PERSPECTIVE OF VALUE

In today's marketplace buyers of all descriptions want to get maximum value for the money they pay. While they often talk about their desire to get the best price they can, there is a far greater need and desire—that of getting the hassle out of their life. People today will pay for creative, high-value solutions when it solves a problem for them.

The key is to understand what they value most and then craft solutions accordingly.

The biggest problem companies, executives and sales-people have with their value proposition is the degree to which they are obsessed with their own perspective of value. What matters most is having people who will work hard enough and creatively enough to converse with the prospects to ascertain exactly how THEY define value. It is through the presentation of value-based solutions, seen through the eyes of buyers, that deals get done and relationships are forged! It's up to YOU to put in the time and energy to gather this critical intelligence that secures a sale, insures a long term relationship and multiple referrals.

The reason it is labor-intensive is because all prospects are different and have a unique agenda. If you don't determine what it is, you are just another vendor trying to sell your stuff. You don't want to be perceived that way. Many times you will also have a complex "DMU" (decision making unit.) If you have four people in the decision loop, each with a slightly different agenda, you are involved in a complex sale, and it is up to YOU to sort it all out.

DEFINING VALUE

As mentioned earlier, the most important definition of value is your *prospect's* definition. Perhaps through your exercise of in-depth communications with them you can assist in the expansion of their perception of value. You will have helped them fine-tune their definition which will often provide you with the simultaneous advantage of providing a solution far more advanced than your competitors'.

In our deep dive research (targeted research in this case) for the content of this book, we studied many other experts and authors on the topic of value and observed several very good definitions and perspectives of value. Here are some for your consideration:

> Webster's Dictionary says value is: The monetary worth of something marketable; relative worth, utility or importance; degree of excellence or status in a scale of preference; a quantitative determination of usefulness.

> Hanan and Karp, in their excellent book *Competing on Value*, define value as the added competitive advantage you bring to your customers. They further say "Whenever you contribute to reducing a customer's overall costs, you add to his competitive advantage as a lower-cost supplier. The winner is the supplier who delivers not the highest-quality product, but the highest quantity of customer value."

> Michael Hammer, author of *Reengineering the Corporation*, says "Sales has been curiously resistant to a value-driven process approach. No other area of the business has proved so stubborn."

> Dr. Larry Steinmetz said "Most salespeople are more worried about and focused on price than their

prospective buyers are. They need to focus on the value they bring to the table, and sell that!"

Maister, Green & Galford in their thought provoking book, *The Trusted Advisor*, said "As a valuable resource we might be consulted on broad strategy issues related to our specific expertise, but we are seen in terms of our ability to put issues in context and to provide perspective."

Todd Zaugg, Master entrepreneur and CEO of Matrix Achievement asks his prospects: "Are you more concerned about the apparent price or the cost, effect, and potential outcomes of the overall solution?"

Rackham and DeVincentis in their bestselling book *Rethinking the Sales Force* say "You would expect that the one place where the idea of adding value to the customer would be as natural as breathing would be in sales. But surprisingly, rather than being a leader in the value revolution, sales has been at best a laggard and at worst an active saboteur."

Mittal and Sheth in their book *Valuespace—Winning the Battle for Market Leadership*, say that "Value, not money, is the basic currency of all human interaction."

THE PROSPECT'S PERCEPTION

High performance salespeople not only sell higher volumes of goods, but they often sell those goods at higher prices. How do they do it? I believe it's because they understand what we refer to as, The Value/Price Perspective.

Anytime anyone makes a decision, they consider principally two factors. They consider the perceived value of that product, service or idea. They also have a mental image or perception of the price which they should pay.

The more skill a salesperson possesses, the less likely it is that he or she will be at the mercy of price. In this chapter, we want to share with you some techniques and skills that will help you build a prospect's image of value to the point that price becomes a less significant issue.

In many situations, people will have a mental image of a price that's greater than their mental image of value. When that happens, it is usually a "no sale." That's because people who are psychologically normal usually won't allow themselves to make an affirmative decision if price appears greater than value.

This will occur from time to time to all salespeople. If you are selling products of high quality, there are going to be times when a premium price is involved. You never want to apologize for that. What high performance pros do in this situation is build value. A prospect's perception of value is subjective and, therefore, subject to influence. The good news is that people are more willing to pay for quality and value today than they have ever been!

Keep in mind that a prospect's mental image of value will vary, based on their needs and their perspective regarding price. Every successful salesperson knows that you don't sell everybody the same product the same way. You must consider needs and applications for each prospective buyer.

Perceptions of price involve more than a dollar sign or a specific amount of money. Other factors that impact on a prospect's perceptions include fear of the unknown and the possibility of an undesirable outcome. Convenience, reliability and timing also may be influential.

Anytime you can compete on the most compelling value rather than the lowest price, you will be able to preserve your company's margin and ensure a higher income for yourself. Margin should be taken seriously, because without it companies fail, so don't mortgage your future by trashing your margin. Protect the enterprise of which you are a part.

If your company didn't have you to sell the value of their products and solutions at margins significant enough to stay in business and hopefully to prosper, they could just sell from their website at a much lower price and not have to pay you. Sales professionals need to put forth a concentrated effort on the potential value of their offerings and discover as many creative solutions as possible to impress prospects with the superiority of their offerings.

Since the most important definition of value is your customer's, keep in mind that their needs, wants, agendas and priorities will vary. Identify high level solutions that build the trust and value necessary to get them to open up to you and share exactly what they value most. When you know a prospect's preferences and needs with depth and detail it will enable you craft extraordinary presentations that really hit the mark. The story below illustrates this principle well.

MY OLD KENTUCKY HOME

The best example I've ever experienced of building value came after I'd had the opportunity to address the annual meeting of Jockey International. You know, the underwear people. Don't snicker—in most of my audiences Jockey products will invariably be very well represented!

I did an after-dinner program with about 700 people for Jockey International in Chicago. They were a positive and responsive audience. A few weeks later I got a phone call from a man who said, "Don, I heard you speak at the Jockey meeting, and you were terrific."

"Thanks!" I said. "You must be with Jockey."

"As a matter of fact, I'm not," he said. "I was a guest at that meeting. Actually I'm president of a firm that's one of Jockey's major suppliers. The chairman of the board of our company and I heard you, and we are interested in our people hearing your message." What followed was evidence of the fact that he was a great listener and communicator who had not only picked up on what my wife's hobby was, but also my interest in aviation.

He said "Don, we want you to come give that same talk to our people at our annual meeting on Saturday, September 22nd. Can you make it?"

Now I love to sell dates on a calendar as much as you love to sell your products or services. But when I looked at my calendar at the date he mentioned, I knew there was going to be a problem. The Saturday he wanted came at the end of a week in which I had six speaking appearances scheduled in six cities in five days. I was to leave town at 5:30 on Sunday afternoon and not get home until 11:15 on Friday night—a grueling week. So I can tell you that, at that point, my mental image of the value of earning one more speaking fee that week was pretty low, and my mental image of the price I would have to pay was very high.

vP

I had made a pledge to my kids years ago that anytime I was out of town all week long, I'd try to be with them on the weekends. It looked as if the price I would have to pay was greater than the perceived value of the speaking engagement.

So I said to him, "You're gracious to invite me, but that is a really tough week and I don't see any way I could make that date. However, I have a lot of friends in the business, so why don't you let me get you another speaker this year and use me next year?"

He said, "Don, let's not give up so easily. Didn't you say in your talk the other night that your wife is into horses?"

"You've got a great memory," I told him. In my talk I had said that years ago, my wife and my secretary got into the Tennessee Walking Horse business. For me, it was like supporting a heroin habit! He remembered that line.

"Don," he said, "would it intrigue you to learn that we are having our meeting this year at the 5,000-acre horse farm outside of Lexington, Kentucky that belongs to our chairman of the board?"

What is he doing to me here?! He's building my mental image of value, is he not?

vP

I said, "5,000 acres? That sounds incredible, and I know it's got to be a beautiful layout. But it's my wife who is into horses. She doesn't normally travel with me. And the truth is, I'm allergic to horses."

Did this slow him down? Not in the least.

"Don," he said, "as I understand it, the problem is that on that Saturday, you need to be with your family. Is that the problem?"

"That is indeed the problem," I told him.

He said "Is that the only problem?"

I said "Yes, it is."

"Well, let me try this one on you for size," he said.

This guy was good! He even remembered my interest in aviation from a story I told in the previous speech.

"Tell you what," he continued. "At 10 o'clock on that Saturday morning, if you and your wife and kids will be at the Memphis International Airport, we will send our company Learjet down to pick you up." The value is now building!

vP

He continued, "It's only a 40 minute flight in the Learjet from Memphis to Lexington. Then we'll get you and your family off the jet and put you on our Jet Ranger helicopter."

"Now Don," he said, "Here's the question I want to ask you, and want you to ask your wife: Have you ever experienced a cool, crisp early autumn morning in central Kentucky? When you get into the Jet Ranger helicopter, you climb about 300 feet and all you see is a hint of fog and some clouds on the horizon. But then you climb up 600-800 feet and the fog miraculously dissipates. And as you look across the horizon, you begin to see those rolling bluegrass hills... white fences... prancing racehorses on their morning run. Have you ever seen that from 800 feet in a Jet Ranger helicopter, Don!?"

"Not lately," I said weakly. (You must know that his value-building exercise was working like crazy with me.)

VP

"Don," he continued, "we'll get you over to the meeting to do your program. Afterward you can stick around for our social activities if you're so inclined. When you and your family are ready, we'll put you back on the chopper. You, your wife and your kids will be back to the Lexington airport in short order, back on the Learjet and back in Memphis by 3:00 that afternoon!"

VP

I felt like saying, "Let's book the program. Forget the fee!" Of course I didn't say that. Never cut price when value is there, right?!

One of the best ways to initiate the value-building process is to find out what turns somebody on and give it to them! When the price seemed high to me, the man made the value seem higher. That's what selling is all about: Getting inside people's heads, giving them what they need and what they want, focusing on value and presenting it with good strategy. That is what gets people to respond. Incidentally, it was a tremendous trip!

FOUR TYPES OF VALUE POINTS

As you craft your offering and prepare to make your presentation, it is time to focus on the value points you plan to present to that prospect. There are four types:

1. **Generic Value Points**—These are the value points your marketing department might have created in an effort to show how your offerings are superior to the competition's. They are generally well received as nice to have and good to know about. You need to know these backwards and forwards; if you do not know the uniqueness and impact of your value; you cannot price or sell it.

2. **Targeted Value Points**—These are the value points that you have facilitated the creation of, and are particularly compelling to this particular prospect as they are in synch with the prospect's definition of value. Perhaps you crafted these with the help of your prospect and someone else

who is in the loop, but the prospect sees them as right on point and highly valuable to them.

3. **Discovered Value Points**—These are the value points which emerge through the prospect learning about the unique application of your solution. You know there is a discovered value point in play when the prospect says something like "You mean if I put this feature in the mix and couple it with this application I can get these (identified) efficiencies?" Anything you can do to help your client discover or extract new elements of usefulness from your solution will usually pave the way for you to enjoy increased sales.

4. **Engineered Value Points**—These are the value points that can have great meaning and impact on the decision-making process. These come into play when you have displayed your creativity in a combination of valuable ways, like...

   a. Listening intently to your prospect articulate their problem and giving careful in-depth thought to how you can be a resource to him in creating a solution.

   b. You get all the info you can and formulate early ideas on what might be done in solution development, and you (for example) go to your engineering department and fine-tune a component for a special application that solves their problem. The more you involve the prospect in this process, the better, as they see creative engineering (that will, perhaps, give them a competitive edge) unfolding before their eyes they really like what this is going to do for them.

c. Many times you bring other people into the loop and tap the collective intellect of say, six people, three from your company and three from the prospect's company and you work together cooperatively and gain consensus on the direction you are going to create a compelling solution for them. This is collaboration in the truest sense of the word.

d. Differentiated value points—These might be value points your competitor also has in their arsenal of benefits, but you have a better version or greater quantity than they do. In the next chapter, *Separating Yourself from the Competition*, you will learn that there are multiple types of differentiation and the more creative you are in bringing them into the mix in a manner that your prospect is impressed by, the better. These help you answer the question "How are you different from and better than the competition?"

Here's an example: Let's take a washing machine. Store A's washer price is considerably higher than Store B's. The customer is trying to figure out why they should pay the extra $300. But because the unit at Store A is of superior quality, part of the price includes an extra three years in the life of the machine. It also includes better washing quality, more efficient use of detergent, multiple settings for less wear on the fabrics, the peace of mind that your clothes will be cleaned well, and not having to put up with the problems that frequently occur with the washer at Store B. And the warranty and repair service at Store A is far superior to that of Store B.

In the end, Store A's washer will be a better buy because of the value the salesperson presents. It's important to understand, however, that part of the value of Store A's washers includes superior customer service and a trust between the salesperson and the buyer. It is up to the sales professional to present the value components in a compelling manner.

You have got to know your value and its potential to sell that value to your prospect. Occasionally, using the above value points, you will be able create a new perspective of value for your prospect resulting in a powerful competitive edge. The better you are at figuring out ways to expand your value points, the more compelling your ultimate value proposition.

THE VALUE CHAIN

The value chain begins with **value premise**. This is generally created by the top management of a firm who makes the decision as to how you are going to market. Somewhere in between the absolute lowest price provider of the company in your sector and the highest price provider in the marketplace is where your company will be.

A CRITICAL PRECIPITATING EVENT

So you eagerly attend your National Sales Meeting in January when the awards for last year's performance will be given and going forward strategies will be revealed. The Senior V. P. of Sales and Marketing gives an impassioned address on how we are going to market in the coming year and beyond. He says "At our senior executive strategic planning meeting last month we made the decision that we are going to market with the absolute best and most differentiated product in our market at the highest price out there. We need each of you to be the best you can be in selling the value of our exceptional offerings, and showing our customers how we are going to help them succeed! The balance of our meeting will be about updated information on our exceptional product offerings and role-play training sessions focused on how you can sell them. Best wishes for a great year!"

Most of the salespeople are slumped down in their chairs saying to their neighbor "Man, this is gonna be hard."

Of course it's going to be a challenge! Most worthwhile gains in life are hard to come by, but this scenario displays the challenges of today's marketplace and how much commitment will be required to excel. Selling value is not for the faint-hearted! It is for the winners who are excited to discover new ways to expand and enhance the customer's experience by building value and solid relationships. Their focus is to help their customer make an informed decision and become their trusted resource. It is for determined, focused, creative professionals who truly want to succeed by helping their clients succeed.

The value premise your management has put in place has defined the environment you will be in as you progress into your territory. Here's our recommendation: Go up to your boss, and say "Megan, I want you to know that I am aware of the challenges we'll have in this competitive environment, but I'm buying in to the vision. You can count on me to give it my best shot to help us win business!" Managers love it when they know you have *bought* in.

The Value Chain

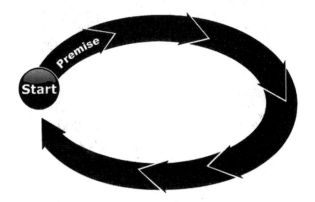

Value Proposition:

The next segment of the value chain is the ***value proposition***. Your value proposition represents the collective benefits of doing business with you and your company. It is up to the sales professional to do an exceptional job of articulating all that you have to offer in terms of value (with all four types of value points being considered) that you bring to the table.

The value proposition, when properly presented, will uncover features and benefits that were not apparent early in the discussion or needs analysis. Incorporate unique features and differentiators into your value proposition for maximum impact. The more tailored and targeted your solution is to that prospect's needs, the better you will be received.

The Value Chain

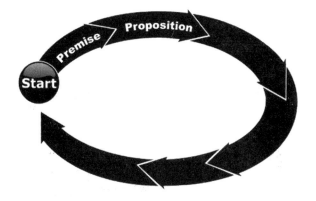

Value Expectations:

The next element in the value chain is *value expectations*. This occurs when your prospect is evaluating the degree to which you really listened in the needs-analysis discussions, and crafted an exceptional solution to their problem. Clarification of expectations is critical to your success. When done properly, you can even expand expectations and create new ones based on the capabilities of your team and your solutions.

The Value Chain

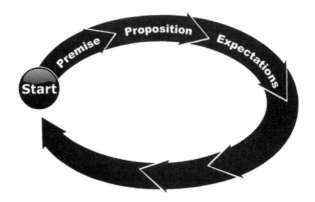

Value Alignment:

Next is the *value alignment* component. It defines the degree to which your proposition and the expectations in place resonate with them and their specific needs. Is your solution, as presented, a compelling way to deal with their most significant problem? If it is, you are competitively aligned to gain the business.

The Value Chain

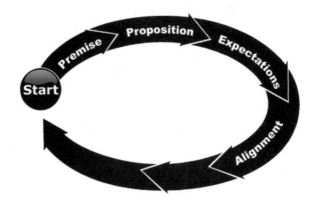

Value Delivery:

Then we progress to *value delivery*. Implementation can be very tricky because there are often so many variables, elements, and personalities involved. Part of your job is to orchestrate the delivery of your solution in a manner that exceeds your client's expectations. (See "Experiential Differentiation" in the next chapter)

The Value Chain

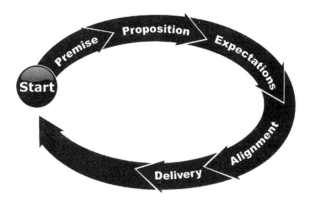

Value Reinforcement:

The final component of the value chain is **value reinforcement.** This is when the results of communication skills shine as we follow up like a pro and continue to assist the client in getting the maximum benefit from our solution now in place. Here are some ways we can solidify and reinforce what we have provided for them in a manner that creates competitive leverage going forward:

1. Check with the client firm to be certain that the application of your product is being correctly and profitably utilized. For example, this may require you getting permission to go into their plant with their personnel to assure quality control or that special skills are being used in their manufacturing process. We have done business with medical device firms where the sales professional even goes into surgery to assure the proper installation and utilization of medical devices.

2. After successful usage for a time, you secure testimonials from the user buyer about the exceptional results they have gained from the inclusion of your solution in their products.

3. Right after the alignment and delivery phases, communication is particularly important. Remember, it is okay to over-communicate, but not okay to under-communicate.

4. Handle the reinforcement phase in a manner that keeps your contacts happy and convinced that you are a valuable resource to have on hand. You want to be well-positioned for the next sale.

The Value Chain

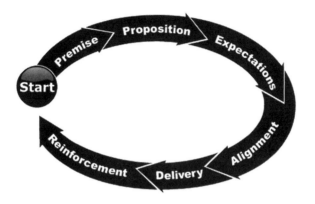

The value chain will help you keep in perspective how you can best develop, define and deploy great value for your clients. As we implement high quality, high value solutions in the marketplace, exceeding your customer's expectations, your reputation and your brand thrive.

Priceless

Identify customer needs and what they value better than your competition does. Gather information from as many of the decision influencers as you can so that you can craft unique value-focused solutions ... by their definition.

CHAPTER TWELVE

Presenting Your Value Propostion

"Present all three dimensions of value: product features and benefits; your company's value-added services; your personal commitment to serve them."

TOM REILLY

BUILDING VALUE IN YOUR PRESENTATION

The best proven strategy to build value in the prospect's mind is to talk benefits. To best address the benefits as the customer views them is to focus on their *needs-based* benefits. This area of focus is based on what *that prospect* needs at that time; and targeted benefits associated with *their definition of value.*

In our earlier chapter on needs analysis, we learned how to ascertain what people are truly looking for. We build value by showing how our product, service or idea can satisfy those needs. Our value-based presentation should feed back to the customer needs-related data that was gained in the needs analysis.

If you don't know how to establish and build value, you'll be faced too often with the alternative of cutting price.

IT'S SHOWTIME!

In preparation for presenting your value-focused solution you have already participated in advanced questioning skills and active listening skills, so you should be primed to get your head into the game of defining and building value. It requires an intense focus on each prospect's unique set of needs, and the willingness to think creatively in crafting personalized solutions if we want to be perceived as extraordinary.

When you perform an in-depth needs analysis for a prospect, and then create a tailored solution that impresses them, you will thrive as a professional salesperson. This is the real VALUE people are really looking for!

Let's explore with more depth today's value proposition, and how it will be presented, so that you can have an approach that is better than all the Tom, Dick, and Marys that have called on them lately!

What can you do that really sets you apart? Set yourself up as one who has a unique approach. Early in the relationship you focused on statements that resulted in them saying, "Hmmm, that sounds interesting, if you could make that happen we might be able to do some business." This is an indication that you are advancing the buying process by offering unique solutions that meet their needs. You are now positioned to deliver a strong presentation.

Before we get too creative, let's be sure to avoid the top five mistakes in presenting the value-based approach. They are:

1. It takes too long to develop and articulate—too boring before you get to the promise.

2. So many value propositions are too internally focused—too much of a "Look at us" approach.

3. Presented in too much of a convoluted process—remember that simplicity sells.

4. Your approach sounds canned—which to them means it's the same thing you tell everybody.

5. It's not customized to their industry or their specific needs to a compelling degree.

The value-based presentation itself should be highly impressive! Make it as special, high-impact, tailored and memorable as possible. You want it to be the best they've heard in a while. The most important single rule to remember is that professional salespeople never give their presentation until they have done their due dili-gence, their needs-analysis, and have established multiple value points to incorporate into a tailored solution. The reason is that if you do a stellar job in the needs analysis, your discovery functions, and value point creation, that will result in you actually delivering a presentation your prospect HELPED YOU DESIGN. That's the one they will respond to!

Noted presentation skills speaker/trainer, Patricia Fripp says "Let get real. Nobody gives a darn about you or your product. It's all about what it will do for them!" That is a smart way to look at it and get the focus off of us and where it belongs—on the prospect.

There are many key facets of information gathering that lead up to the culmination of the process. Don't over-look any of them because you need to identify where their dominant buying motive lies. You need to know what it is so that you can develop an on-target presentation.

Here are seven key recommendations for designing and delivering a successful presentation:

1. Be certain you have talked to all of the key deci-sion influencers in advance so that you can incorporate tailored data from each of them into your presentation. If you are using PowerPoint you might even put their verbatim quote on a slide with attribution to them. The higher they are in the pecking order the more powerful the impact.

2. When you can, manage to get to the senior executive who was responsible for this area to be present for your presentation if possible. One good way to have that person in the loop is to start there in your sales call process.

3. Create/craft and incorporate specific value points to advance your tailoring process.

4. Be sure you are giving the presentation to the right person or group with all decision-influencers on hand if possible.

5. Creatively tie their senior management's philosophy into your presentation when you can.

6. Make your presentation fresh, dynamic, pertinent, and well organized.

7. Involve them interactively whenever you can to maximize involvement, engagement and discussion.

The meeting to present your solution will often be a success, not necessarily because you are a hit, but because your process for presentation design is right in line with their needs, wants and priorities. You can do the same thing time and again in slightly different ways with different prospects, but the key is to dig deep for valuable information you can use to maximize the impact and pertinence of your presentation.

Presenting Your High-Impact Solution

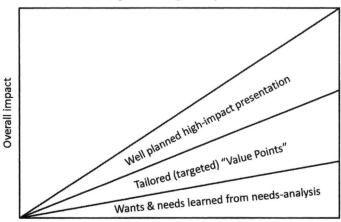

High-Impact components crafted for presentation

THE NEEDS-BASED PRESENTATION

Have you ever known a salesperson who had "I" trouble? That's a person who goes into a presentation armed with too many "I" words: "Let me tell you about what I... me...we..." This is a salesperson asking for disappointment. Prospects consider such conversations extraordinarily boring. High-performance salespeople don't have "I" trouble. They go into a presentation focusing on the prospect they want to serve. Their favorite word is "You".

When you focus your conversation and energies not on yourself but on your prospects and their critical issues, you are on your way to positive results. When you get into the prospect's head and identify their needs and dominant buying motives, you have positioned yourself to give a higher-quality presentation than ever.

HOW TO GET IN THE "NO FAIL" ZONE

No matter how great your product is, if you let yourself get preoccupied with what you want to sell instead of directing your focus on the needs and problems that have already been articulated by your prospective buyer, you are in trouble. Your presentation will not be good enough to get a "Yes" and you will compromise your conversion rate and disappoint your prospect.

Your presentation to each prospect should be designed based on your knowledge of what your product can do for *them*. But even more importantly, you need to focus on what you've identified and agreed on as the customer's need. If you have a professional needs-based sales approach that focuses on what you learned in your information gathering process, giving the presentation that your prospect helped design will not only be a smart approach, it will dramatically increase your chances of getting a "Yes." You need to be so aware of the needs and desired results of your prospects that you never ask them to do anything that is inconsistent with those needs and desires.

To make a presentation based on your prospect's needs, you must be very aware of your prospect's agenda. In today's marketplace, we don't give "pitches." (I really dislike that word—it implies you are going to slickly pull their strings or manipulate them into a yes.) The word is presentation today, and the viability of your presentation will be based on the research you do, the creativity of applying your capabilities to their needs, and crafting an excellent presentation that will make the difference.

THIRD-PARTY IMPACT— THE POWER OF IMPLIED ENDORSEMENT

The best way to help a customer make a more comfortable decision to work with you is through the power of a trusted third party. When you share your past successes, either verbally, in print, or online, in a tasteful, low-key manner that are supported by a third party, the accolades appear more authentic and trustworthy. Testimonials on LinkedIn, or in your online or offline marketing, can be helpful in giving your prospects the confidence they need to make an informed decision that leads them to take action. The more those references relate to their problems and needs, the higher the impact they'll have.

In their excellent book *Strategic Selling*, Miller and Heiman said, "Having a guru or an R&D expert tell a prospective buyer that your company is at the cutting edge of a certain technology may be a much more effective way of getting your message across than your saying, "We have the best stuff on the market." This is a great way to demonstrate your abilities from concept to application.

The power of implied endorsement through authentic testimonials helps the customer make a buying decision when they observe the contacts and businesses who are willing to post their testimonials online.

THE BENEFITS OF THE INSIDE INFLUENCER

Let's discuss the "inside influencer" and the trial presentation. The inside influencer is an individual with whom you have a special relationship and a special communications link. I have benefited from several such relationships through the years. These were people who really wanted the company to buy our training and willing to help any way they could to assist me in gaining the commitment from management. Your inside influencer will tell you more than others within the organization might tell you. They will be very frank as to what people want and need and what others are thinking about your offerings. The inside influencer can be extremely valuable to you in the process of putting together a proposal that hits the mark.

Smart salespeople often make a trial presentation to their inside influencer. This presentation should be informal, confidential, no visuals, just verbal, with cursory details. Take the opportunity to run it by them before you give your formal presentation. Ask for specific feedback. Say, "Sue, would you let me give you a rough idea of what my presentation will contain, and see how you feel about it before I formally present it to the committee?"

Here are some tips:

- Present the material to your inside influencer in an informal fashion.

- Evaluate their response and ask how they think others on the committee will respond. What are the individual feelings that might be expected as a result of that presentation and the concepts being presented?

- Ask about any "hot buttons" you may be overlooking.

- Get a commitment from this person not to discuss this offer with other key people before your presentation.

- You may want to withhold some facts or numbers in this trial run.

HAVE A CONSENSUS AUDIENCE

A key to getting the yes in any sales effort is to have every decision maker and decision influencer present for your formal presentation. A presentation without these key decision makers is can be a waste of time and effort.

Remember, that you may be dealing with subordinates that have the power to say "No" but don't have the authority to say "Yes." To win the sale, be sure to recognize and respect this veto power.

In some situations, you may be better off to just simply ask, "Mr./Mrs. Prospect, would you be the decision maker in this area, or are there others we'll need to get approval from?" Be careful not to come across as pushy or offensive here, just try to find out. Often you can learn who the decision maker is by asking a knowledgeable third party.

Another idea is to present yourself (and/or your firm) as one which does some consulting. Inform your contact that there is no charge for needs analysis research, information gathering, and program (or presentation) creation. You do however; need to ask that all decision makers and influencers be on hand for your presentation. This is a reasonable request and may give you positioning for a presentation to some key people who might otherwise be unavailable to you.

YOU TELL ME, I'LL TELL THEM

Should you encounter a situation like this, be ready to restate your offering, because this is a bad deal! The prospect you are talking with wants you to do a lot of work but is circumventing your access to present to the decision makers. This is not a win-win situation. In a number of instances, I have declined to do the initial research under these conditions. Here are some strategies to handle this situation:

- Consider your options, think about and evaluate your position carefully when a similar situation arises, because that prospect cannot and will not effectively present your product or service for you (even if they promise to do so!)

- Ask if there is some issue to presenting your services to the decision makers.

- Ask questions to drill down to the real problem the prospect is facing.

- Offer to provide your presentation information in alternative formats (i.e. Skype, Shared Screen, conference bridge lines, etc.)

- Regain your position by stating that you would be interested in offering solutions to the company's needs at a time that is convenient to meet with all decision makers.

- After careful evaluation, without access to the decision makers you may make the decision to walk away.

PROJECT A POSITIVE TEAM IMAGE

Don't ever refer to your manager, your company, or its executives with the word "they." Use "we" to project a team image. To use the word "they", has a negative connotation, and it implies a lack of commitment as well as the absence of a team spirit at your firm. It can take the punch out of your presentation. Always speak in a positive and favorable way about your company and about your immediate superiors within the organization when possible, as it creates and conveys an image of a solid, cohesive working unit.

PRESENTATION UNIQUENESS

Your goal is to make every presentation unique. The observant salesperson should be able to make each presentation a one-of-a-kind experience because each individual prospect's problems and priorities are unique. Encourage that prospective customer to participate in the design of the recommended actions. You can do so by simply asking a prospect's opinions and monitoring their responses throughout the interview.

In a sales situation, you should not be involved in an attempt to dominate and control, but rather engage in a free-flowing exchange of information, and a clear understanding of needs. The result should be that the prospect's trust in you is high and, they will seldom reject you. The customer will openly advise you of what's getting in the way of a positive decision so you can better address any problems in a win-win way. It is a proven fact that the sales presentation which focuses on solution development can be a unique opportunity for you to set yourself apart from your competition.

There's a certain feeling, a special camaraderie that develops when you present your ideas in a manner that specifically and creatively addresses a prospect's needs. Make some references in your presentation that are so specifically and perfectly directed at your prospect's company that they will know for sure you have designed this just for them.

ASSESS MOTIVES

You presumably have done a professional job at this point of identifying and clarifying your prospect's needs in the development of a sales presentation. Be sure, too, that you've always done a thorough job of identifying the buying motives of each of the decision makers and decision influencers.

A motive is defined as an emotional impulse which causes one to take action. Nothing is more frustrating than giving what you perceive to be a great presentation, only to get an indifferent response. When this happens, it's usually because the presentation missed the mark and didn't focus on the client's dominant buying motive. It is possible to address need without addressing motive, so be very careful here. Anytime you can, address both. You're positioned perfectly for getting the "Yes" when you do.

Keep in mind that the presentation process should not only focus on client need and motive, but also follow a logical, high-impact sequence. Ask yourself these questions

1. Have I established rapport and trust?

2. Are all of the decision makers present?

3. Have I clarified the decision-making criteria and their value points?

4. Am I benefit- and solution-oriented in what I'm about to propose?

If you answer "Yes" to all four questions, you'll be hearing many more "Yes" answers from your prospects. Your goal is to get firm, positive decisions at the time of your presentations, but sometimes it doesn't all come together as we had hoped. A solid effective proposal and presentation process can help you a great deal in getting timely decisions.

HOW TO PRESENT SALES PROPOSALS

One major deterrent to gaining positive response in a timely manner is that many salespeople simply give their quotation or proposal to their primary contact and leave. Their plan is to await a decision that is to be made at some future point. When we take the simple path of least resistance, we often shoot ourselves in the foot. Try to avoid this pitfall in the sales process.

The highest performing salespeople figure out creative ways to keep the sales cycle short. One way is to do everything in your power to be present when the decision is made. You can dispel the prospect's doubts, remind those in the decision loop of important value-building benefits, and keep enthusiasm high regarding your tailored solution and the service your prospect will get with it. You can also offer input that justifies urgency and a timely decision. If you are at the mercy of some vague group made up of people you haven't even met, you are an accident looking for a place to happen.

ORGANIZING YOUR PROPOSAL

A proposal can be a powerful means of presenting your ideas and gaining the buyer's commitment if it employs the right structure and is presented in the most appropriate sequence.

Ron Willingham, an author, friend, and expert in this area, once told me about a simple, well-thought-out structure designed to lead smoothly into an affirmative decision from your prospect. He suggests we call our presentation a "Proposed Action Plan" rather than a proposal. He recommends that we organize the proposed action plan into four sections.

The first section would be entitled "Client Profile" and would have three subtopics, as follows:

I. Client Profile

A. Type of firm

B. Size and makeup of firm

C. Previous and current experience (in your area or product category, or an elaboration on the previous appointment and actions to date.)

In my area of services, the "previous and current experience" would concern training. For a widget salesperson, it would be widget procurement history. In this area, you would feed back the information you gained in your needs analysis. The more detailed and accurate this section, the better. Strive to make the information succinct. The more complex and lengthy a proposal, the more cumbersome the decision-making process becomes. Try to find the fine line between appropriate thoroughness and fire-hosing them with needless data.

II. Client Needs:

The second section in your Proposed Action Plan would be "Client Needs." Add the appropriate number of subtopics according to the needs you determine. It's best if you can condense and categorize the needs into six subsections or less, so that this section fits on one page. Make a list of the top two to four client needs which will vary by client...

A.

B.

C.

Again, you are feeding back the data you gained in the information-gathering process and adding your specific recommendations as well. Make the wording of the various client needs match as closely as possible the wording and direction your prospects used when you talked with them. If you perceive a need the prospect was unaware of and you want to list it, that's fine—but don't make it first. Add it further down the list.

III. Solutions and Applications:

The third section will be the "solutions and applications" section designed to address the needs outlined in Section II. This is the area where you can articulate your recommendations. Make your recommendations as specific and benefit-oriented as possible, and including multiple value points. Your prospects often need to be reminded of some of these items previously discussed, and there may be people present who were unaware of some particular benefits you are now carefully articulating. Next would be your list of solutions, applications or options (these will vary by client).

A.

B.

C.

You may want to follow up with the A, B, and C in your solutions section corresponding directly to the A, B, and C in your needs section, but sometimes this is difficult. You may have spotted five needs but will recommend only three solutions, due to overlapping positive results with certain solutions.

IV. Investment and Terms (These will vary by client)

A.

B.

C.

You will want to make this the last page you hand out. With this strategy, you have had time to build your audience's perception of value, talk benefits, and impress (influence) them with your research, preparation, dedication to service, before mentioning price. (Tip: Use the word "investment" instead of the word "price".)

To complete your proposed action plan, prepare the customary signature section in which the prospect approves your proposal.

Tip: Ask the prospect to "approve" the agreement rather than to "sign" it. The word "approve" creates a more authoritative position for your prospect and mitigates the thought of a "contract" transaction.

HOW TO BEST PRESENT GROUP AND COMMITTEE PRESENTATIONS

To become a high-performance salesperson, we must learn to make effective presentations in a group setting. There are three vital ingredients for great presentations before a committee or group. Those ingredients are pertinence, preparation, and impact.

1. Pertinence

For the best outcomes, in the opening moments of a group presentation, regardless whether you are addressing three people or ten—share some data with the group that lets them all know unequivocally that you've done your homework and done it well.

Let them know that the presentation they are about to hear is completely pertinent to their situation or problem by saying: "In my data-gathering process and research, I learned some interesting information about your company, your specific needs, and your management philosophy. One of the things that impressed me most was your vice president of manufacturing's premise that ... Then give the relevant quote "......".

From this point forward, you refer to other elements that reveal to your audience beyond the shadow of a doubt that they are listening to a presentation designed specifically for them. Yes, get into the detail and the information that applies specifically to their operation. You may even want to pull a reference from their company's mission statement that reinforces some of the ideas and principles you present.

If you are on target in presenting ideas truly pertinent to their company, their current needs and their philosophy, they'll be impressed. They should walk out of that meeting muttering to each other, "Boy, she really did some in-depth research and tailoring." Chances are you'll walk out with the sale.

While these ideas are relatively simple and obvious, 90 percent of today's sales proposals still have too much "we" and "us" and not enough "you" orientation. How long will it take for salespeople to learn this? Who knows?

2. Preparation

The first tip regarding preparation is to always be early for a group presentation. Check your environment to be certain that everything you will need is on hand. Make sure the room is set up exactly as you want it to be for maximum effectiveness and impact. If you'll be using audio/visual equipment, check it in advance. Don't leave anything to chance. Additionally, do whatever you can at this point to minimize interruptions and distractions.

Have you ever had a little stage fright? It's normal, and some constructive tension can work in your favor. The more presentations of this type you make, the better your presentations are likely to become. *The Book of Lists* states that the number-one human fear is not death by burning or drowning, as some might think. The number one fear is speaking before a group! Most of that fear is unfounded but, whether founded or not, if you are nervous and fearful as a speaker, you have to deal with it because it will be very real to you at that moment.

Speaker Cavett Robert had an excellent observation on fear and nervousness before a group. He said, "Even after years of speaking, you never totally lose the butterflies—you just learn how to get them to fly in formation!"

Well, how do we do that? Be so well prepared and well-rehearsed that you know it's going to go smoothly. The best insurance for a confident, successful group presentation is a strong knowledge of the topic coupled with a high level of preparation.

In getting ready for a presentation, try to anticipate what your prospects want and need to hear in order to respond positively. Try to anticipate any apprehension and present ideas to eliminate it. And, as we have already discussed, be sure your focus is on the needs of the organization and the individual decision makers.

3. Presentation Impact

To have impact you want your presentation to be different from and better than what they are used to experiencing. Make it well-prepared, well-timed, and present the unique factors in it with conviction and flair. Include and demonstrate various items that are non-traditional and effective to capture and keep their attention. Examples might be to use online presentation platforms, video, or interactive screen to screen selling software to engage their attention that is unique and to best demonstrate strong differentiation.

Another important idea is to selectively choose the proposal pages you distribute at the start of the presentation. It is better to not distribute the proposal with all pages intact. This strategy ensures that they cannot turn to the back of the proposal to look at pricing. If they turn to the back to see the numbers first you risk the chance that your presentation will be preempted.

To best maintain control of your proposal presentation, distribute the proposal one page at a time focusing on the content on that specific page, fielding questions, etc., then hand out the next page. If you have a six page proposal to present to three decision-makers, go to the meeting with six manila folders, one for each page of the proposal—nothing stapled or clipped together. Take extra copies in case others attend the meeting you hadn't planned on.

Begin by giving each person a page one, go over it, then give each person a page two, and review it, answering any questions or facilitating discussion along the way. Continue this process until you are done. This will enable you to build and articulate the value before you get to the investment. I've used this approach dozens of times and it works very well.

GENERIC ADAPTABILITY: HOW TO CAPTURE EVERYONE'S ATTENTION IN YOUR PRESENTATION

You can often assume that in a group presentation you'll have people from each of the four behavioral style quadrants on hand. If so, then you will want to say things in your presentation that appeal to all four behavioral styles. If you have as many as eight or ten people in your audience, it's a good bet that you will have at least one from each quadrant—Driver, Expressive, Analytical and Amiable. Here are sample statements to use before my audiences:

"We are here to discuss increasing your profits today through learning and using the latest value-based selling skills" (appeals to the bottom-line orientations of the Driver)

"I hope, during the course of this presentation, we'll have some fun and, at the same time, really get into the motivation of what will make you a higher-producing sale professional!" (appeals to the dreams and excitement desired by the Expressive)

"But I don't want you to think I'm going to concentrate so much on helping you become motivated that I neglect the intricate details necessary to make the training process effective. So right now I'd like for you to open your workbooks so that we can cover the data you will need to be your best" (appeals to the detail orientation of the Analytical)

"When we conclude this program today, I hope we will have not only improved our skills and had an enjoyable experience together, but also learned how to have better business relationships" (appeals to the needs of the Amiable)

That's an example of generic adaptability. What did I do? I used a sentence or a phrase or two that appealed to the value systems of people in all the various behavioral styles.

By learning how to tailor our group presentations to all behavioral types, we're becoming more adaptable and responding to the needs of all of our listeners. What does that mean to us in the marketplace? It improves our results and thus our income. Everybody wins.

> **Priceless**
>
> **Make every presentation a creative work that is as much about the client as about your solution. Be certain your presentation impresses them with the fact that you are a unique and valuable resource to them!**

CHAPTER THIRTEEN

Separating Yourself from the Competition

"If you want to move up, you've got to stand out!"

TOM PETERS

THE DYNAMICS OF DIFFERENTIATION

Your ability to differentiate yourself from your competition is based largely on your ability to demonstrate to your prospects that you and your company are different in your approach to solving your clients' problems. Few things are more important to salespeople in a competitive marketplace than your ability to do this and do it well.

Think out of the box in this discussion on differentiation, because you need to stretch your perspective to be refreshingly different from the salespeople they talk to every day. In their eyes you want to be a category of ONE!

Picture your biggest, toughest competitor, the one you lose business to more than anybody else, and then ask yourself this question: "How am I telling and showing the marketplace that I am different from and better than them?" If you can't come up with a good answer in ten seconds you are in trouble because you are not paying enough attention to differentiation.

Go about discovering what it is you can do to differentiate how you and your offerings are perceived in the marketplace.

- Are you selling a commodity? If it is purely a commodity and you are not doing anything about presenting uniqueness, then you are absolutely at the mercy of price.

- Don't ever put yourself at the absolute and total mercy of price. It is not profitable and it is totally unnecessary.

- Be a pro in differentiating what you are selling. A commodity is a product or service without distinguishing characteristics that is available from multiple sources. Unsophisticated marketers believe that there are two types of differentiation—product and price—and two only.

Some people today have the deadly mindset that there are a lot of companies that can provide your marketplace what you are providing, so you are going to have to be the low-price provider or you are not going to get any business. This is a terrible mindset. It reminds me of a book that Zig Ziglar's brother, Judge Ziglar, wrote entitled *Timid Salesmen Have Skinny Kids*. The message is: We can't be timid. We don't want to be arrogant, but we can't be timid about how we go to market and how we articulate our differences.

There is a lot more to it than our offerings and the price we charge. If prospective clients can convince themselves that what you're selling is something that they can get from many different places, they can be comfortable in the mindset that the only thing that matters to them is price. So while they are busy commoditizing your offering you need to be busy differentiating it in every creative manner in which you can. Tell the marketplace how your solution is different, better, creative and superior.

Share with them all the benefits that you and your company bring to the table. That's the power of differentiation. The marketplace doesn't need any more *me too* folks in any business. So creatively differentiate to be exceptional. In this chapter you will learn about our U.S. Learning Differentiation Model which has seven types of differentiation. Use as many of them as you can to create your uniqueness and stand apart from the crowd.

Even if you are selling a commodity, you will learn from this chapter how to be perceived as exceptional. Your ability to go to market as a differentiated entity with value and benefits that your competitors do not offer is critical today.

SEVEN WAYS TO DIFFERENTIATE YOURSELF FROM THE COMPETITION

We've determined through our studies and consulting activities that for most businesses and services there are seven types of differentiation. Let's examine each. Give careful thought as to how each type could be utilized in reference to your own offerings.

1. Product Differentiation

How is your product or offering superior to your competitors'? If you can't come up with some solidly unique components, you may be in danger of being perceived as just another commodity in the marketplace. Here's a strategy: Perhaps a think tank or special committee within your company can make product enhancement a major initiative. Have people on the committee from multiple disciplines to gain wide and variable input. You might even want to include a good long-time customer. Together you can brainstorm and discover unique features about your product or service, or create new ones, then creatively exploit every aspect of the difference and tie it into what the prospective customer values.

Your goal is to come up with both UCAs (Unique Competitive Advantages) and RAs (Relative Advantages). This gives you admirable positioning in your marketplace and impresses your prospect base. Do anything you can do to make sure that your prospects see you in a positive light that is directly tied to THEIR BENEFIT for maximum resonance. Seek excellence in the delivery of your presentation to your prospects as you point out the excellence of your product.

2. Relationship Differentiation

When there is a solid relationship between you and your clients based on high levels of trust, you have an inside track of tremendous value. When they respect and trust you, you have created an environment that will be the envy of your competitors. In fact, the client may not even give your competitor a chance if your relationship is strong enough. Build that trust with a solid, high integrity, win-win approach by exceeding their expectations and being a valued resource in every conceivable way. Be prepared to invest the time, perseverance and appropriate activities to earn their trust.

My colleague and long time friend, Dr. Tony Alessandra, author of *Non-Manipulative Selling*, said "If two people want to do business together, the details are probably not going to get in the way. But, if either one of those two people does not want to do business with the other, the details are probably not going to make it happen." That's the power of a positive win-win relationship.

Have you ever had the occasion to be sitting at your own dining room table with a salesperson who has called on you? The experience gravitates into a negative scenario whereby they asked you for the order before they had earned the right? Your stress goes up and your trust comes down as you feel the pressure. It quickly becomes apparent that this guy has got a severe case of "Commission Breath." Our goal is to create high trust relationships that bridge the trust gaps to allow us to stay connected for long after the sale for repeat business and endless referrals.

Most of the top performers we interview understand the value of "investing" in relationships to secure long term business from it while being a trusted resource to the client. When you understand the power of relationships, you lock out the competition regardless of changes in the marketplace. Your competitors won't know what hit them!

Implement creative ways to keep in touch and to add value through both online and offline platforms to keep the relationship fresh.

A few recommendations that have worked well are:

- When you've established a relationship, find out the date of your prospects birthday. Instead of sending an email or posting on Facebook, consider sending a greeting card through the mail.

- When you see a news tip or magazine feature that can help their business or features a positive write up about what they do, scan or copy and send to your client with a short note "thought this would interest you" or "congrats on good press!"

- Don't miss keeping in touch online. Discover what online channels they prefer to frequent and use their preferred form of communication for regular consistent "value touches".

Relationships that are nurtured on a regular basis will to grow.

3. Experiential Differentiation

Experiential differentiation is more than just good customer service and simple customer satisfaction.

A hefty percentage of today's consumers is influenced by the "experience" involved in their engagement with a product, service, salesperson or company. As an example, the GenX/Y segment of the consumer matrix is all consumed with the experience of the purchase. A good example is Starbucks. It's clearly not about the coffee, but what buying the coffee provides as an experience. You can order a coffee 19,000 different ways to suit your preference. Starbucks offers not just coffee, but a "community" that is encouraged to "commune" at their locations, and seduced with free Wi-Fi, music and the exposure of socialization. You can easily drive through any McDonalds and get a coffee, but in this case, the consumer will pay for the "experience" that accompanies the purchase.

It's performing miracles and making people say "Wow, those people at Acme are fantastic to do business with!" When you provide people with great experiences, your reputation begins to spread like a prairie fire on a windy day.

Many people believe that we are in an "experience economy." Can we provide customers with experiences that are so memorable that they start telling their friends and neighbors? This element of "viral" communication goes beyond marketing when the customer offers their implied endorsement of your product or services without being asked.

Outperforming your competition is another way to gain market share. Find out what your customers' expectations of service are and do everything in your power to exceed them. Continually amaze them with delivering before promised deadlines and prompt response to even the smallest of issues, and they will give you more of their allegiance.

Some people don't care about what kind of service they provide. They just want to put the numbers on the board. That may work for a little while, with some companies. But when you start chipping away at your customer base because you have delivered marginal or slow service, your days just might be numbered. It doesn't matter what the number cruncher in the CFO's office happens to think, when you chip away at your database with marginal service, you will eventually burn through your customers. One of the greatest ways you can gain allegiance to your organization and thus to you individually is to do everything in your power to deliver a great experience for them.

4. Process Differentiation

Don't have processes locked in stone. Be willing to do some frequent tweaking and fine tuning when we can to keep customers happy. Be able turn on a dime.

Many companies don't attach enough significance to the processes that dictate the image of their business model. Most personal and business behavior is based on habits. The "but we've never done it that way" syndrome bites us in our profit zone when we don't give innovative thought to how we do business. When we do an excellent job of listening to our customers, we receive input that is strategic to us in terms of process improvement. Have you ever had a client say "Megan, if you could get your accounting department to get our invoices and statements to us so that we receive them by the tenth, we could not only get you paid faster, it would also work better with our accounting process"?

Get your best minds together and brainstorm better, more customer-friendly ways to do business. Think out of the box and do some things that have never been done before. Your customers will be impressed with your spirit of innovation and your team members will become more energized in the process. Remember that how business is conducted changes every day due to globalization, e-commerce, the Internet, new software programs and of course, technology. Do some internal selling when necessary to make your colleagues aware of customer preferences.

5. Technological Differentiation

This age of technology affords many opportunities to advance our ways of manufacturing technically superior products and operating at previously unheard of levels. New modes of communication encompass a wide variety of options, from using podcasts, text notifications and video email reports to update customers, or address customer-sensitive issues, to a blog that allows "voice" and interface to "hear" from your customers that result in the advancement of your prospect understanding of updates, changes and timely buying opportunities.

A key factor to excelling in today's marketplace is to adapt to the buying preferences of Generation X and Y, which requires providing technologically-savvy ways to speed up the ordering, shipping and delivery processes. Get your best technological minds together to brainstorm how you can make technology work to impress your prospects and customers with speed and convenience 24/7. Today there are many ways we can make it easy for the customer to communicate and buy.

Addressing the different core values of each of the four generations will propel you to top sales. It's a smart strategy to survey your current and past customers with their preferences. This data will give you the information you need to tailor your business and communication process to meet and exceed their expectations. Remember, you can buy a book in every town, but Amazon.com is a giant today because they make it easy, safe and 24/7, so follow the leaders! Communications technology has always been key, but learning the customer's preferred channel is critical. Here's an interesting example:

I had a man in a seminar recently, and as we were discussing the "DMU" (decision making unit) he said "Don I'm often involved in a complex sale where I am selling more than one person, like a committee of four for example. Just last week I had such a situation and the contact person assigned to me was a young twenty-seven year old guy who won't return my phone calls. I've called him three times, left messages and have yet to get a response!"

I said, "Let me see if I have this straight. He's your contact and he's representing the decision making unit, you have a lot at stake, with a big potential sale. He's twenty-seven years old and he won't return your phone calls?"

He said "right!"

And I asked, "How old are you?"

He said "Fifty-seven".

I said "Why don't you try smoke signals it works just about as well as a phone call with a twenty-seven year old."

If you do not know how to text you are out of business with prospects in that generation. We have got to have the technological capability to communicate with people in any means and manner they prefer. If it's tweets or texts before 7 AM, give them their desired response, in desired media, before 7 AM.

6. Marketing Differentiation

Give careful thought to how your brand is positioned in your market. I have seen some companies that had "me too" products but were creative enough in their marketing to prosper. This creates a powerful difference in your marketplace if you incorporate a sales and marketing approach that is unique and engaging, clearly differentiating you from your competitors.

If everything else you are offering is exactly like your top three competitors, so be it -just outsell them! When you can outsell them, you get the business. How do your selling skills compare with your competitor's selling skills? Boost your skill sets by studying sales leaders online daily and by following top influencers on YouTube or through blog posts. How is the sales training of your company compared with the sales training your competition is doing? Even if your company is not offering training, seek out online tips, sign up for RSS feeds with valuable insights on the latest engagement and selling tips.

Learning in terms of advanced selling skills will enable you to incrementally improve your skills. If you can out sell them you are going to get the business, all other things being equal.

Marketing also consists of public relations, advertising, social media communication in addition to selling skills! Stay on the cutting edge on all fronts.

Determine ways to create a distinction in your marketing that supports setting you apart in your marketplace. If your differentiators are compelling enough, are presented articulately enough, and in synch with what your prospect values, you will render your competitors and their product or services *irrelevant!*

Use technology to create a competitive edge. Consider deploying a successful Internet marketing approach that opens your marketplace to attract prospects in all age groups and demographics using tools like a free trial offer, or a downloadable coupon.

Design your direct-mail advertising campaigns to include web responses and free reports compelling enough to receive an above-average response and to track the effectiveness of your campaigns.

Study your market and find out what everybody else is doing then do something different! Whatever you do, do it differently and better than your competition. Adding value added services that capture attention and foster engagement is your goal.

A sure way to garner more customer attention is to market your offerings that provide something special for your customers that they don't expect. Everybody loves a little "extra" or small premium, gift or valuable information that says: "We care about you, value you as a customer and care about your satisfaction."

Want to really blow them away? Bring them a solid lead for their business! Helping them grow their business is guaranteed to have them gravitate toward you. Find out what they want and need and provide it for them with creativity and an edge. Use personal notes and don't forget that although email is a terrific medium, not everybody uses it properly or frequently, so never underestimate the power of a simple handwritten note. It works like magic!

7. Price Differentiation

Unsophisticated sales and marketing people often think that the best way to get business is by underpricing everybody else. So they trash their margin, buy business, and then wake up only to realize that they can't make any money that way. Thin or non-existent margins have put more companies out of business than any other single factor. If you choose to go to market as the low-price provider, you better have every expense category cut to the bone, including sales commissions, or you will perish in short order. In my opinion, this is the worst avenue of approach in trying to build a viable long-term enterprise. When you are competing with giants in your marketplace, there is no way you can continue to cut into your profit and stay in business.

Now, let's talk about the flip side: pricing at the higher end. The executives at Rolls Royce Motors have no interest in being the lowest price in any category. They know what they build and sell is special and that people are willing to pay for it. Their exceptional products and prices have survived for over a century, so it is apparently working for them.

There have been many stories related to companies which increased their prices only to see their products fly off the shelves. The psychology of pricing can be complex, and we won't address it here. Just know that in today's world there are many people who are willing to pay more for a superior solution that will provide them the superb value they want and save them from hassle or inconvenience. Keep in mind, too, that we can often make a case about perceptions of price that can be very convincing.

Know the difference between *apparent price today* and *ultimate cost over time*. This story below illustrates how we can make this vital comparison work.

Will Schulte, a salesman at Chromcraft Furniture, called on the national headquarters of a rental company to present their seating line. His goal was to become a primary supplier for the company's rentals to businesses.

Will knew their seating was a good 20% higher than the product the rental company was carrying. His approach was to build his presentation on the quality and performance of the Chromcraft product in order to justify the additional cost.

At his first meeting with the company, Will realized that this sale was not going to be easy. Price, as he had anticipated, continued to be the primary objection. But he knew how attuned this company was to bottom-line profit as a major consideration. Even after several unsuccessful calls on the buyer, Will persisted in looking for the right button. Then he hit on a way to let the facts and figures do the selling for him.

He did an analysis based on the rental company's records of replacement costs, repair costs, and life of the chairs they were using. He compared these figures with records on Chromcraft's chairs used in specific large installations.

When this analysis was laid out to the decision makers, Will made his sale. He showed the rental company that, even though they were paying less for our competitor's chairs, they were really paying more. With Chromcraft, they would pay less in returns and repairs and enjoy a longer rental life. And the real icing on the cake came later for the company, when the resale of the Chromcraft chairs after several years of rental turned out to be higher than the company was experiencing before.

Within a short time, Will turned that company into one of the largest purchasers of Chromcraft seating in the United States. And he did it with a quiet, simple and very effective technique: he dazzled them with the details and showed them what real value was.

Priceless

Creative differentiation, properly presented, can be like a new oil patch for you and your company. Use the collective intellect of the people in your firm to figure out how to go to market in an exceptional manner that rings the bell of your customers like never before!

CHAPTER FOURTEEN

Getting the Order!

"If you can't get commitments, you can't sell."

Don Hutson

OBJECTIONS ARE OBJECTIONABLE

For decades the topic of objections has had a negative connotation. The general perception has impacted the salesperson and the sales process negatively, when in fact, it is quite the opposite! Objections can be excellent buying signals.

Objections are a positive sign and when you understand the psychology behind the "why" of their push back, with the right communications, you can help your customer get to the decision making process.

We can start with the wording itself. At U.S. Learning, we prefer to replace the words "Objection Handling", with a more positive view and refer to it as "Addressing Prospect's Concerns", eliminating the stigma of the word OBJECTION. This chapter lays out a recommended process to help you address the concerns that slow would-be buyers on their way to a decision.

Handling objections makes it sound as if we are going to manipulate them to our way of thinking. Dealing with a concern positions our services as a way of helping them solve a problem. We have found that there are essentially four types of concerns.

1. Stated—This is good! You want the prospect to spell it out for you, and the more detail the better.

2. Unstated—These aren't so good. It usually means that they don't want to open up and share their agenda with you. It is tough to deal with a concern you don't know about.

3. Implied—Sometimes we can discover valid concerns from passing comments and non-verbal clues that prospects make. Be sure to verify the accuracy of your assumptions on these.

4. Unknown—These are concerns which have not emerged as yet, so we need to be alert for them when they do.

Be thankful when they put their concerns on the table, because if they don't bring them up we can only guess what their apprehensions are. Build trust, ask questions, and learn all you can about their issues. Keep it positive by presenting yourself and your company as problem solvers and solution providers. Confidently go into your chosen formula for dealing with concerns and listen for additional ones as a prospect shows signs of interest.

THE RECOMMENDED FORMULA

We developed a proven five-step process for dealing with manageable concerns. When you utilize this strategy to its best and full potential it will clear the obstacles that get in the way of getting an order. It is non-confrontational and comfortable for the salesperson and the prospect. And it is easy to remember—we call it the A-E-I-O-U formula. Just remember the vowels and it will help you go through the process effectively.

- The "A" is for attention. Give them your full attention with a willingness to listen and listen respectfully. Block out all distractions and get into the game with them.

- "E" is for empathy. Put yourself in their shoes. Not sympathy; sympathy is "I feel like you feel." Empathy is "I understand how you feel," and you can go there psychologically without being totally sympathetic. When you have empathy for their situation you will be able to identify with their challenges and help them develop solutions.

- "I" is for investigation. Get to the meaning of their concern by asking them why that might be an issue. Probe for details so that you can gain understanding and identify the key issues bothering them.

- "O" is for overcome. Your goal is to help them clear the hurdle to get this done. There is no confrontation in this process. It is about working together to create solutions.

- "U" is for update. Make sure that the concern is behind them and that they are ready to proceed. If they are not, they will customarily tell you. Sometimes you will need to go back through the five steps again.

Be glad they shared the concerns with you. Sometimes the toughest person to sell is the one who never says anything. They may give you some nonverbal communications from time to time, but if they don't say anything you don't know where you stand. I would much rather have someone who is voicing concerns than remaining silent.

Don't skip any steps because that will short-circuit the process. Once you get used to it and use it a few times, you develop the habit and you will have it down. Expect some discomfort at first, as you would in learning any new skill set. Comfort comes with continued use.

GAINING COMMITMENTS VS. CLOSING THE SALE

Once again, we have re-named this skill with what we feel is an improved term. Instead of "Closing the Sale" we call it "Gaining Commitments." The philosophy is simple. We are beginning a new relationship when we gain their commitment, we are not CLOSING one. The essence of selling, ultimately, is the ability to facilitate a decision to buy. That means getting people in the right frame of mind to make the commitment to go forward. This skill is designed to help you do just that.

If you do everything properly leading up to decision time, you have a great shot at getting the YES you are looking for. The reason you need to learn all of the steps presented here is that you don't want any weak links in your sales process.

Keep in mind the importance of earning the right to ask them to buy. The early sales trainers who used to say "The only way to find out the best time to close is by attempting to close too soon and too often!" would fail miserably in today's marketplace. That may have been a viable idea many years ago, but not today. Remember the lessons in the "Evolution of Selling" —stay away from high pressure! Using the right selling style today will help us earn the right and earn more business with success and proficiency.

A consultant and friend of mine, Don Thoren, was retained by a sales organization a few years ago to come in and help their salespeople improve their conversion rate. They were simply not getting orders like they felt they should. Don worked with them for weeks, but surmised early on what the problem was. They were not asking for the order! They were talkers. They thought they were doing and saying the right things as they talked about benefits, but they were NOT asking commitment questions.

They were initially offended when he gave them his diagnosis. But he videotaped his role-play sessions with them and they were astounded to learn that he was right. They were not asking commitment questions. Don't fall into this trap. You will sell more when you are highly proficient at asking commitment questions, at the right time and in the right way. Role-playing, for commitment question skill-building, is a great way to improve your proficiency.

MENTALLY PREPARE FOR THE COMMITMENT PHASE

As you approach the commitment phase, you are entering the hallowed ground of decision-making. If you handle it poorly or inappropriately in any way it will become apparent that you are in quicksand. This is one of the most sensitive areas in the selling process, and you must handle it with great care if you want to excel. Ask yourself the question "Have I earned the right to ask for their business at this point?" You earn the right by professionally performing your due diligence to include your needs-analysis, the identification of their value definition, and the necessary research to assure that you have the best possible option for them.

Sometimes a problem will surface because the prospect simply doesn't want to do business with you or your company. When this happens, it usually means either they are uncomfortable with you personally or they perceive your actions or suggestions to be inadequate or inappropriate for their needs.

If they think your presentation is too product-based and feel all you want to do is close them, earn a commission, and go on down the road, you have gone bear hunting with a pea shooter. Your commitment-gaining skills will usually be inadequate because your sales approach is substandard. Hopefully, successfully performing the skills we've previously discussed will keep this from happening.

These possible roadblocks simply underscore the premise that every part of the selling process holds potential for losing the sale. If the previous steps and activities in the selling process have been professionally performed and have contributed to a strong foundation, the decision will often be the logical result when you reach that magic moment.

Many salespeople perform one or more parts of the selling process in a sloppy way and then they're amazed when things go wrong with their attempt to get the commitment. This often occurs when the salesperson asks for the order before building trust with the client. The old ABC cliché (always be closing) is no longer viable in today's marketplace. Any salesperson who asks for business before earning the right is chipping away at any chance of building trust.

GOOD TIMING AND
TRIAL-COMMITMENT QUESTIONS

Timing can be everything in securing decisions. When the natural communication flow is present, you will often get verbal or non-verbal buying signals that indicate the prospect's readiness to make a move. Capitalize on them, and get the prospect's commitment while you can.

High performers are masters at spotting windows of opportunity to make the sale. If you don't get a specific verbal buying signal, look for any positive indication that the prospect is convinced of the value of your offer. Be confident and assertive, but don't be pushy.

One way to ascertain whether it's appropriate to close at a particular point is to ask a trial question. It can be a casual question like, "Do you feel we're heading in the right direction to try to solve your problem?" If the prospect agrees you're on the right track, you will want to attempt to get an affirmative decision soon.

Other examples of trial questions would be, "Huey, do you think we're going to be able to do business?" Or, "Kristin, does this appear to be a solution that is responsive to your needs?" The simpler and more casual, the better the trial question.

To attempt to get their decision before earning the right is like knocking on a turtle's shell to get it to stick its head out. It seldom works. Read your prospect carefully for their response to your ideas and proposals. If you ask for the business too soon and get a negative response and keep on selling, you are faced with the difficult task of getting them to swallow their pride and change their mind. Use trial questions to assess their feelings. Remember that more assertive people have shorter attention spans and less assertive people have longer attention spans, requiring more time. Build trust early, keep stress low, and you'll sell them sooner and with less difficulty.

IMPLIED SUPERIORITY, WITH HUMOR

A friend of mine, Lou Pera, owns a commercial roofing company. At every opportunity he introduces me to someone as the world's second-greatest salesman, with the obvious implication. We both laugh and I let him get away with it.

He was recently talking to a prospective client about a new roof for their plant and was getting some strong price resistance. So Lou said, "Let me ask you a question (followed by a long pause). Are you going to put anything important in this building?" The prospect started laughing, and, as you might guess, he bought. Maybe Lou is number one.

COMMITMENT TECHNIQUES

Now, let's assume you have earned the right and you are ready to ask for the business. I think you need to have several commitment techniques in your repertoire to make the process smooth and comfortable for both parties. Here are eight commitment techniques.

1. The alternative choice—This one has been around for years, and continues to work very well. It is essentially the "don't ask if, ask which" approach. Simply give them a choice, either of which includes them buying from you. "So Mr. Robinson, would you prefer we ship to you via truck line or FedEx?" When he answers, he has bought.

2. The time-sensitive tactic—This is an excellent approach if you are able to use it without pressure or manipulation. You say, "Eric, I'm delighted you have interest. I'm going to ask for your permission to enter this order today— our inventory shows we only have 220 boxes remaining, and your order is near that. I don't want them to get away and cause you delays. Is that okay?"

3. The forceful summary—This one does especially well with the analytical buyer. You forcefully, comprehensively summarize. First you restate the three main things that your needs analysis indicated are priorities for them and then you state three corresponding solution elements in your recommended deliverable. This can be very convincing.

4. The casual commitment approach—This is when you casually attempt to get their commitment with non-threatening verbiage such

as "How does this sound, Karen?" When they respond positively, they have bought.

5. The boomerang technique—This is when you give the reason they give you for NOT buying as the very reason why they should. It might go like this: "Dr. Green, you mentioned the 2% higher investment with our proposal. This is a miniscule amount of money when you consider that the product life cycle of our pumps is 20% greater than the other options you are considering. For that 2%, you are getting an enormous ROI from our quality!"

6. The direct question—When you get a buying signal like "It appears that you have covered all the bases with your proposal this time" you say, "That's great, Scott. Should I write it up?"

7. The assumptive action—When you get a buying signal or a positive comment, you assumptively say "Excellent, Rebecca. I can get you in our delivery system this afternoon." You then present the paperwork.

8. The automatic decision—I love this one. It's when the sale miraculously confirms itself! It's when the salesperson is interrupted with "Lisa, you've told me enough. I'll take it." All you have to do is let it happen. Don't say "Wait a minute; I'm not through with my presentation yet!"

We've covered some excellent alternatives for you to use to get orders. I want to ask you to practice, drill and rehearse these tactics to get commitments. You are only as good as your reflex actions, so learn them well and they will be at your disposal when you need them.

MAKING A CREATIVE SALE IN THE FRACKING INDUSTRY

I want to share a story from one of my clients, Schaeffer Specialized Lubricants, that shows how creativity and patience can turn a big sale into an even bigger one. The term "fracking" has been in the news a great deal lately for its application to drilling for natural gas. It is the process of drilling and injecting fluid into the ground at high pressure to fracture shale rocks and release natural gas inside. With roughly half a million natural gas wells in the United States, it's a huge, transformative business.

Schaeffer's sales team led by Chris Dix had been working for some time with a client, Superior Well Services. Here's how Steve Brewer of Schaeffer tells the story.

We were presenting data we'd collected on an application that had been challenging for the customer for years. The data was quite detailed and showed that our product, which in this case was a gear lubricant, delivered measurable and significant performance advantages.

After our presentation, Superior asked us if we had any technology that we could bring to the table to address another, even more challenging, lubrication problem. Along with the rest of the industry, Superior had struggled for years with the packing lubrication for the frack pumps. This packing is exposed to extreme pressure, contamination and load. Conventional lubricants had failed to resolve the issue and created environmental and logistics challenges to boot. Although the products were relatively cheap, they did not perform well and were mainly used because they were readily available and inexpensive.

At a break in the meeting, Chris and his team began to brainstorm. When the meeting resumed, we announced that we had designed a unique new approach to the application. Rather than using a traditional "fluid" approach (which requires vast volumes of product at low cost and has severe environmental collateral impact) or a traditional "grease" approach (which delivers adequate lubrication but has challenges in cold temperature), we utilized a proprietary hybrid formulation that tripled the life of the packing while reducing the amount of lubricant required by nearly 70 percent. The solution was provided at a price that was higher than synthetic greases that were being used, but the product pumps at very low temperatures and is available in a biodegradable form affording value more significant than the additional cost.

This outside-the-box, thinking has taken nearly three years of field trials and reformulation as well as an extraordinary investment by our company. But the product is now beginning to be accepted in the industry. We got Superior's commitment on a large sale and are now on our way to additional sales based on what we learned. Nothing was fast about this sale, but it will be huge for us over time."

The best way to close a sale is to have a relationship of such high trust that your customer never gives any resistance to your recommendations.

Priceless

CHAPTER FIFTEEN

Maximizing Relationships

"Most people can discern the difference between a salesperson who is out to make a dollar and one who is out to make a difference."

TODD DUNCAN

LEVERAGING RELATIONAL CAPITAL

Someone once said "It's not what you know but who you know that really counts!" I would never refute the importance of knowing the right people, but I would suggest that there is something even more important than that. It is who knows you and what they think of you. What kind of grade do you give yourself on developing solid, win-win relationships with people who can help you?

In a seminar recently one of my audience members said "Don, isn't leveraging a relationship manipulative?" It was a good question. I said "No, unless you plan to do something dishonest or untoward. If you believe in yourself, your company and your solutions, you should be eager to provide the value and benefits you have to offer." Manipulation implies the likelihood of a win-lose outcome.

I heard of a woman recently who was a top sales professional who told a mutual friend that she has worked very hard in recent years to expand her network, and thus her influence. She was very proud of her track record in leveraging social media to meet new people, and in passing, mentioned that she had 900 people on her Christmas card list. Wow, that's impressive. Most people know about three to four hundred people. I can see the value of gaining new friends, especially if you are in a business where you can leverage those contacts successfully. It apparently worked well for her.

I mentioned in an earlier chapter the fact that I introduced a client in the floor-covering business to a client in the hotel business. The companies were multi-billion dollar corporations, and they did a lot of business with each other after my introduction on both sides of the relationship. Both people were friends. I was willing to leverage my relational capital for them. This is an excellent example of how to build and advance relationship differentiation.

This introduction and the business they gained from it enhanced their image of me and my company. Through this mutually beneficial introduction they both saw me as a friend, but also a very valuable resource to them in a non-traditional way. This gave me a competitive advantage when I presented our training and development solutions offered by U.S. Learning. Such differentiators can build a business.

STRATEGICALLY ADVANCING RELATIONSHIPS

I think you would agree that most of us today are in a relationship business. One of the most powerful skill sets to perfect is relationship advancement. Can you treat this skill as a separate, serious initiative, that we nurture and master, by giving it our constant time and attention? I believe that if we do, we will be on our way to internalizing one of the great methods of building a bigger book of business, along with longer lasting, profitable relationships.

If you develop good daily habits you will soon be among the top five percent of people in sales today. This skill will help you compress more achievement into a given measurable time frame quicker than anything else.

The key is to master the process, then use it every day. Through the power of the daily compound effect, you may wake up one day rich in relationships, and in cash!

Joe Gandolfo wrote a book with a great title: *Ideas are a Dime a Dozen, but the Man who Puts Them Into Practice is Priceless*. It's not what we know, but what we do with what we know that matters most. Don't ever miss an opportunity to advance a relationship. Since few things, if any, are more important in your sales career than advancing relationships, develop the habit and discipline to do these things on a daily basis, and your career and your earnings will soar!

GAINING VALUABLE REFERRALS

One of the most valuable habits you can develop to advance your sales career is asking for referrals. It has been proven that referral prospecting is the most powerful but underused means of gaining business in the marketplace today. Your goal should be to develop a process that you are totally comfortable and confident in using every day.

The best people to ask for business are usually your existing customers. The higher people are on that Loyalty Ladder, the greater the probability they'll come through for you. If they are pleased with what they have bought from you and the service you've given them, they'll normally be happy to give you leads and allow you to use their name when contacting them.

I want you to get more referrals than ever. Here's the recommended procedure: Build the request for referrals into an appropriate place in your sales process, after you have established trust, and use it consistently. Here are eight tips that will help you gain referrals.

1. Make asking for referrals a standard part of your sales process. Most salespeople forget to ask, and, frankly, really don't have a confident approach. It is too important an opportunity to be casual about your process. Adopt a mindset

that enables you to develop it, test it, perfect it, and use it with every client.

2. Target the best time to ask them for referrals. You don't want to ask too soon. Use trial and error to figure out at what juncture in your sales process works best for you. Then ask every time it's appropriate.

3. Build trust and earn the right to ask. When you reach the point that you are comfortable asking, by that time they are usually comfortable in giving them to you.

4. Target a group from which they can refer you. Make it easy for the client you are talking with to think of a prospect for you by suggesting a group or "center of influence" that produces results. You might say, "Mr. Dillard, who do you know in your purchasing club that you think could benefit from knowing about me and the solutions we provide?" Get as much information on the referral as possible and follow up promptly. Use the referring party's name only if you gain their permission to do so. Don't be reluctant to ask for it. Here are some "thought starters" for groups to target:

- His golf foursome.

- People in their service club.

- Others on Boards of Directors on which they serve.

- People from industry groups.

- Those they go to church with.

- People on their street.

You get the drift…any group they are a member of might (depending on what you are selling) be worth targeting.

5. Delegate getting the appointment. The late sales trainer Fred Herman said the best way to get a referral and appointment is to simply ask someone to get it for you! Tell them when you are available and get the person you are seeking the referral from to go ahead and get you an appointment. It's gutsy, but it often works. You might want to say "Kevin, do you think you could get me a face to face with Arthur Brooks? I'd really appreciate your help on this." Once in a while they'll say, "I'll call him right now!"

6. Use an effective "bridge statement" as you transition to the referral discussion. Here's one my friend Bob Burg, author of *Endless Referrals*, recommends: "Karen, I'm in the process of expanding my referral network and I find it helpful to partner with friends like you. Can we take a few minutes and run by a few names of people who I might be able to help?"

7. When you get a really strong referral, such as "You tell Brad I told you to call on him and I said he needs to work with you," you can use

the "asked-promised technique." It works like this: "Brad, Stan Evans asked me to call you and I promised him I would. I'd like to arrange a time when I could come by and talk with you about your needs and our offerings."

8. Use the "principle of reciprocity" when you can. Let them know that you are willing to help them get new business. Ask them "If I were to tell others about you and your offerings, what words or phrases should I use in describing what you do for your customers?" This is an implication that you are willing to help them get business, and it makes it a lot easier for them to help you when you ask for referrals later.

Remember that the success of the ideas outlined above is largely dependent upon your ability to create and nurture high-trust relationships. In the absence of trust, you will usually be in a relationship that has underlying stress which is not conducive to asking for and getting referrals.

With the rising costs of making sales calls, this prospecting technique becomes more valuable to you every year. The payoff on sales calls is increased when you can leverage solid relationships into additional leads through a viable, perfected process. Use the words that you have found work for you, have the confidence to ask, and choose the perfect time to do it. When you implement these tactics, there is an excellent chance that you will be able to increase your list of good prospects substantially. Remember too, that making warm calls tends to get us better response than cold or new ones do!

PRESIDENTIAL WISDOM

When our National Speakers Association Convention was in Washington D.C., one of our influential members got the board and past presidents an audience with then-President Bill Clinton at the White House. It was an experience to remember. When President Clinton said "Now tell me what it is that you do," a few of us chimed in with terms like keynote speakers, business trainers, and motivational speakers. He said, "I see. I think I'm in the same business most of you are in! It seems like I spend half of my time trying to get people in the right frame of mind." It was a poignant observation that shows how attitude and relationships really do make the difference.

POSITIVE RELATIONSHIP SKILLS

Some refer to positive relationship skills as people skills. There is a good bit of ink devoted to how we handle relationships in this book, and I make no apology for it. You can be totally motivated, have more product knowledge than anyone else on your sales force, but if your relationship skills are marginal, you will be a marginal producer. We are all in the people business, and President Clinton was right about the importance of getting people in the right frame of mind. Through good adaptability skills, a positive attitude, creative use of humor and cutting edge interpersonal skills, you can lead your sales force.

Many managers today suggest that it is best to hire for attitude and teach the skills. In some industries requiring substantial technical expertise that might not fit, but generally I agree with this premise. It is much harder to teach positive attitudinal skills than product knowledge in most cases. The more likable you are the better you will do in your quest to be a trusted advisor.

GET PUMPED!

Selling isn't easy. There is no sugarcoating that. Sometimes the challenges seem impossible to overcome. To end the final chapter of this book, I will share with you a story that shows how even a toxic relationship can be turned into a profitable one by a sales team with patience, determination and skill.

Centro is a company that supplies industries in nine southern states with valves, steam products, pumps, compressed air controls and process instruments. In 2006, Centro bought out BAT Pump and Supply in Arkansas to expand its product line and sales. One of Centro's targets was a large chemical plant that had not previously done much business with BAT Pump. What Centro soon learned was that the chemical company had a terrible relationship with one of their vendors that was now going to be doing business under Centro's brand.

When Centro President Mike Gallagher went to a vendor conference he got an earful. And when he and account manager Ken Jones visited the chemical plant they got another earful. The bad feelings, to put it mildly, went both ways.

"They listened for a few polite minutes," said Gallagher. "And then they informed us that they HATE the vendor and will NEVER buy from them. They love Centro and like BAT Pump and they're glad we put the two companies together, but they're never going to buy pumps from us.

"So Ken and I are standing in the parking lot and Ken says things look pretty bad. My response is "Ken, this will be great, because nobody thinks we can be successful and we are going to prove them wrong. We are going to leverage our outstanding performance on our other product lines and keep working and waiting for our opportunity. Sooner or later the competition will stumble, or people will change jobs or retire, and when they do we will be there. The only way we will lose is if we stop trying."

Ken Jones evaluated each of the key decision makers at the plant from top to bottom. Unfortunately, three of the top people were the most adamantly opposed to the vendor. But two of them were slated for retirement, and the third was looking at another job. So Jones and his team went to work on likely successors to the big three. They positioned Centro as an alternative and even began to help them out in times of need such as weekends and after hours for the next two years.

Their big break came when a fresh face got a promotion to one of the key decision-making jobs. He added Centro to the approved vendor list and Centro soon captured a big order. Jones used the same strategy with the manufacturer, courting an engineer who had not been a part of the feud and biding his time until the corporate hierarchy changed. It took more than two years and a lot of hard work, but Centro wound up with a big new customer for its pumps as well as several of its other product lines.

Thanks to Ken Jones's skill at maximizing relationships, the companies that once said NEVER now see each other as long-term business partners.

IT'S A WRAP

This book is as much about how you treat people as it is how you sell them. Show them respect, get inside their head, make great recommendations that are beyond their original expectations, and you may just have a customer for life!

Here's the real bottom line: Selling Value is more than a strategy, and it stretches beyond smart selling to being a top responsibility for those sales professionals who want to be an ongoing exceptional resource to their clients.

The real sale happens AFTER the sale and that is where the magic really lies. When you exceed the basic standard of selling a product or service for currency, and strive to create enduring, long term relationships, you are on your way to a lifetime of endless referrals and success beyond your dreams.

We've all heard that "There is no traffic jam on the extra mile." I agree with the premise, and it is my hope that you will work hard to be exceptional in not only the effort you put forth, but the intellect you exercise to utilize the skills in this book.

Winners don't just happen to show up on that extra mile either. They focus, strategize, concentrate, study and learn to be better in all phases of human communication and connection so that their business, prospects, and customers seek them out.

It is my hope that these ideas will impact your strategic approach to selling in a manner that results in a dynamic increase in your commitments gained and monies earned. An audience member asked Jim Rohn some years ago what book he should read to develop his sales approach. Jim said "I would never suggest you make one book your bible, because there many great sales books. Read ten and use the best ideas of each!" This was great advice. We need to continue to look for ideas that can help us advance our expertise.

Top sales professionals have clients who actually WAIT until they can work with them and will refuse to buy from a competitor because the relationship value is more than simply price for a product. You can't buy loyalty. You earn it and it is given to you. And once you have it you realize that it is indeed, priceless!

Priceless

Go the extra mile in building relationships, practicing thoughtfulness and crafting creative, client-focused solutions at every opportunity. Your status as a trusted advisor and valued friend will soar as will your status on the sales team.

Acknowledgements

Making a book come into reality is the culmination of much work and collaboration. I want to express special thanks to my editor, John Branston, a long-time friend and skilled writer/editor who did much more than a cursory edit. John's input was exceptionally valuable and added measurably to the finished product.

Additionally, I want to acknowledge my colleagues at U. S. Learning who helped tremendously in getting this manuscript to the publisher. Kristin Fletcher, my very able assistant, is a master organizer and helped a great deal on the book. And Terri Murphy, our C. I. O., and an accomplished writer in her own right, offered excellent input for improving the book in multiple ways. Rebecca Day, our

Virtual Training Project Manager also offered a new set of eyes when we needed them.

Special thanks to Ken Blanchard, not only for writing the foreword, but for his friendship and substantial influence on how I think about business today. And thanks, too, to his able senior editor, Martha Lawrence, for her untiring efforts in our various projects.

I am also most appreciative of colleagues and clients who assisted with stories and examples which served to reinforce the content covered. These often vivid illustrations and practical applications make for memorable examples of how to apply the methodology in today's marketplace.

Finally, I want to thank my colleagues in Speakers Roundtable (check out www.SpeakersRoundtable.com), for their unending support and encouragement in many ways. The influence of this fellowship has been a mainstay of my speaking and writing career since 1978, and I treasure the relationships.

About the Author

Don Hutson's career spanning speaking, writing, consulting, and sales has brought him many honors. He worked his way through The University of Memphis, graduating with a degree in Sales. After a successful sales career, he established his own training firm and today is CEO of U.S. Learning based in Memphis, Tennessee.

He has spoken to over half of the Fortune 500, is featured in over 100 training films, and currently addresses some 50 audiences per year. He is the author or co-author of thirteen books, including the number one *Wall Street*

Journal and *New York Times* bestseller, *The One Minute Entrepreneur* (with Ken Blanchard).

Don's knowledge and platform experience in selling value, leadership and negotiations have been sought out by companies and associations throughout the world.

Don was on the Founding Board and is a Past President of The Society of Entrepreneurs. He was also on the Founding Board and is a Past President of the National Speakers Association, and a recipient of its Cavett Award for outstanding achievement. He is also the recipient of NSA's "Master of Influence" Award. He is a member of Speakers Roundtable, a think tank of twenty thought leaders in training and development. He is also in the Speakers Hall of Fame.

The Author's Services

Don Hutson and the team at U.S. Learning have decades of experience in training and educating sales and management professionals in many industries. In addition to products like books, CDs, DVDs, etc., Hutson and his company are pioneers in the production and marketing of Virtual Training Programs on numerous business development topics now available online at www. USLearningVT.com.

U.S. Learning offers live convention keynote addresses, training seminars, and consulting services of Hutson and the subject-matter experts on his team.

All appearances are provided after in-depth needs analysis, and are tailored to the needs and specific objectives of each client. The topical areas covered are:

- Basic and Advanced Sales Principles

- Negotiation Strategies

- Selling Value

- Entrepreneurship

- Leadership/Management

- Customer Loyalty

For an initial conversation or to set up an in-depth discovery meeting with Don Hutson or a U.S. Learning team member, contact U.S. Learning at 901-767-0000, at www.USLearning.com, or at www.DonHutson.com

To contact Don, call 901-767-5700, email him at Don@DonHutson.com, or visit www.DonHutson.com.

Now, about your BONUS! First, thank you for purchasing Selling Value. For additional learning, please enjoy a 7-day access into selected chapters of my Virtual Sales Training Program, SELL VALUE, NOT PRICE! by visiting...

www.USLearning.com/SVbookbonus

Thank you and good selling!

Don Hutson

Recommended Reading

Selling with Style
Dr. Tony Alessandra, Don Hutson and Scott Zimmerman

Non-Manipulative Selling
Dr. Tony Alessandra and Phil Wexler

May You Drink from the Saucer
Jac Arbour

Peak your Profits
Jeff Blackman

Raving Fans
Ken Blanchard and Sheldon Bowles

The One Minute Entrepreneur
Ken Blanchard, Don Hutson and Ethan Willis

Endless Referrals
Bob Burg

Flash Forethought
Dan Burrus

Moments of Truth
Jan Carlzon

How to Win Friends and Influence People
Dale Carnegie

Relationship Selling
Jim Cathcart

Profitable Growth is Everyone's Business
Ram Charan

What the Customer Wants you to Know
Ram Charan

Influence
Robert B. Cialdini

The Richest Man in Babylon
George S. Clason

Good to Great
Jim Collins

There Are No Limits
Danny Cox

Innovation and Entrepreneurship
Dr. Peter F. Drucker

Recommended Reading

High Trust Selling
Todd Duncan

Get What You Want
Patricia Fripp

Ideas Are a Dime a Dozen,
but the Man Who Puts Them Into Practice Is Priceless
Joe Gandolfo

The Patterson Principles of Selling
Jeffrey Gitomer

Get Talent
Dr. Paul Green

Reengineering the Corporation
Michael Hammer and James Champy

Consultative Selling
Mack Hanan

Competing on Value
Mack Hanan and Peter Karp

The Kindness Revolution
Ed Horrell

The One Minute Negotiator
Don Hutson and Dr. George Lucas

The Sale
Don Hutson

The Amazement Revolution
Shep Hyken

Selling Value

Strategic Acceleration
Tony Jeary

Life is Tremendous
Charlie "Tremendous" Jones

Lead, Sell, or Get Out of the Way
Ron Karr

The One Thing
Gary Keller with Jay Papasan

21st Century Positioning
Jack Kinder and Gary Kinder

The Runway of Life
Peter Legge

The Trusted Advisor
David Maister, Charles Green, and Robert Galford

The Greatest Salesman in the World
Og Mandino

The Victorious Attitude
Orison Swett Marden (and all others by Marden)

Eloquence in Public Speaking
Dr. Kenneth McFarland

How to Build a Dynamic Sales Organization
Robert N. McMurry and James S. Arnold

Personal Styles & Effective Performance
David Merrill and Roger Reid

Strategic Selling
Robert Miller, Stephen Heiman, and Tad Tuleja

Recommended Reading

Create Distinction
Scott McKain

Valuespace - Winning the Battle for Market Leadership
Banwari Mittal and Jagdish Sheth

World Class Selling
Art Mortell

Release Your Brakes
Jim Newman

The Optimism Advantage
Dr. Terry Paulson

The Power of Positive Thinking
Norman Vincent Peale

Make Change Work
Randy Pennington

The Experience Economy
Joseph Pine II and James H. Gilmore

To Sell Is Human
Daniel H. Pink

The Winds of Turbulence
Howard Putnam

Professional Selling Techniques
Nido Qubein

Rethinking the Sales Force
Neil Rackham and John DeVincentis

The Loyalty Ladder
Murray Raphel and Neil Raphel

Selling Value

Value-Added Selling
Tom Reilly

Human Engineering and Motivation
Cavett Robert

The Fred Factor
Mark Sanborn

The Magic of Thinking Big
David J. Schwartz

Learned Optimism
Dr. Martin Seligman

Nice Guys Finish Last
Lawerence L. Steinmetz

The Success System that Never Fails
W. Clement Stone

Exceptional Selling
Jeff Thull

Success Is a Journey
Brian Tracy

It's the Will Not the Skill
Jim Tunney

Customer Intimacy
Fred Wiersema

The Best Seller!
The New Psychology of Selling and Persuading People
Ron Willingham

Recommended Reading

Prosper
Ethan Willis and Randy Garn

Full Price
Thomas Winninger

Zig Ziglar's Secrets of Closing the Sale
Zig Ziglar